The Democracy Index

The Democracy Index

Sergey Khrystenko

iUniverse, Inc.
New York Lincoln Shanghai

The Democracy Index

iUniverse books may be ordered through booksellers or by contacting:

iUniverse
2021 Pine Lake Road, Suite 100
Lincoln, NE 68512
www.iuniverse.com
1-800-Authors (1-800-288-4677)

Because of the dynamic nature of the Internet, any Web addresses or links contained in this book may have changed since publication and may no longer be valid.

The views expressed in this work are solely those of the author and do not necessarily reflect the views of the publisher, and the publisher hereby disclaims any responsibility for them.

ISBN: 978-0-595-44128-0 (pbk)
ISBN: 978-0-595-88452-0 (ebk)

Printed in the United States of America

Contents

Introduction

The qualitative side of Democracy index depends on what logic is included in it. If there are many objective constitutes in the index which reflect human freedoms, equality before law, freedom of movement, freedom of choice, freedom of choosing a country to live in, etc. In this case, the Democracy index will be objective, will correspond to the real situation of values and services.

I suggest to present index in vector form as follows:

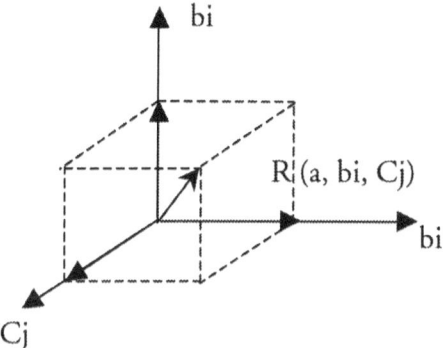

where

   $\pm$ a—the vector of freedom of human

   $\pm$ bi—the vector of equality before the law

   $\pm$ Cj—the vector of brotherhood, mutual—solidarity of country population

$$Z = + a + bi + Cj \text{ - The Aggregate Democracy Index}$$

The research institutes prescribe how to treat our and your Democracy. They suggest a specific "Democracy Mixture" which, in my point of view, can be used only in diluted form.

The reader might ask the question: Which part is missing in the "Theory of Democracy"?

That is, let's say, a small three-volume book in leather binding does not exist:

Volume I—The Economics of the Legislative Power Branch

Volume II—The Economics of the Executive Power Branch

Volume III—The Economics of the Judicial Power Branch

Having such a three-volume book, we would realize what is the economic essence of the state power sphere. But today, as of this moment, we are in a sticky situation. The state power sphere has its headquarters, but the economic theory of the state power sphere is missing.

There will be those who will object to this idea. We will be reminded that on each power branch there are expenses, which are taking into account, and so on.

First of all, taking into account the expenses of the power branches does not mean that the researches have understood the economy of state power: where are the resources moving in the power sphere.

Secondly, it is good that democracy is not a firm subject. On one hand, this is a plus, but on the other hand, it is an obvious minus—the services which are created by the state power sphere are not tangible.

If democracy is not a firm subject, then it may perse something airy, that is ether … yes, yes, yes the ether of human relations which are impossible to touch.

The Democracy index must reflect many sides of the democratic way of organized society: freedoms of people, equality before law, freedom of movement, freedom of choice of the place of living. On one hand, but on the other hand the «Democracy Index» must reflect the economic side of how state power creates into the services of population in the realization of daily rights of ordinary human.

Synopsys

In this book the author examines the specific «Atmosphere of Democracy» which creates seven power branches: 1) legislative 2) executive 3) judicial 4) press 5) Radio broadcasting 6) TV broadcasting 7) Internet.

The author examines power services in the quantity of economic products.

The book will interest all those who create and consume power services.

CHAPTER 1

Three Basic Branches of State Power— Roman Version of State Structure

K. Marx, working on «The Communist Manifesto» introduced for the first time the concept of «basis» and «superstructure».

He identified the superstructure with the sphere of state power. Considered this detached from economic system?

He did not define the essence of the superstructure or specify its system.

He did not examine the economy of each of the branches of state power.

K. Marx studied law to become a professional lawyer, was a practicing barrister. He knew well the provisions of the Roman Law envisaging the existence of three branches of state power—legislative, executive and judicial.

Why he and his followers—Marxists—did not investigate the economic aspect of the superstructure?

Why he and his followers—Marxists—did not investigate movements of streams of resources in the sphere of superstructure, i.e. within legislative, executive and judicial powers;

Why he and his followers—Marxists—did not investigate economic relations in the sphere of superstructure: taking into account the process of production, distribution, exchange and consumption services, taking into account the legislative, executive and judicial power.

It is necessary now to reveal the essence of the superstructure, its component, interaction, binding points and direction of movement of all elements of state power.

According to the regulations of the «Roman Law» the state shall have three branches of power—legislative, executive and judiciary. Guy Julius Caesar, the Roman emperor, compared the three branches of power with a three-horse chariot:

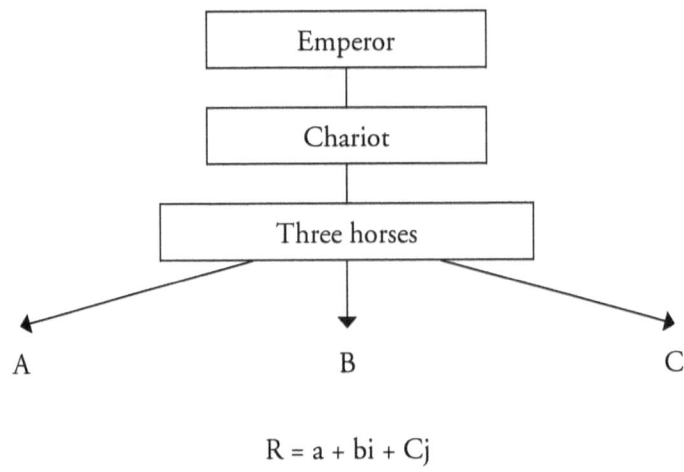

$$R = a + bi + Cj$$

What proportions should exist among the services of the three branches of state power?

How to define the effectiveness of a separate branch of state power?

These questions can be answered only after economic estimates, criteria and indicator for each branch of state power has been elaborated.

I suggest that the three basic branches of state power should be arranged in a three-dimensional Cartesian system of coordinates, as follows:

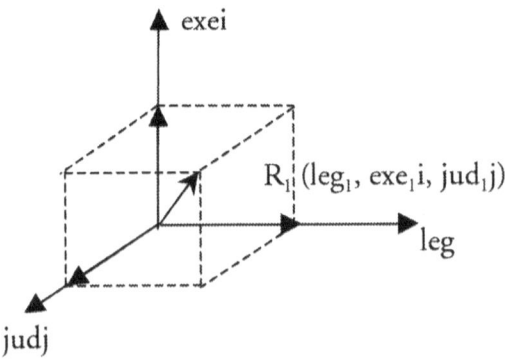

where

> leg—vector of legislative power services;
>
> exei—vector of executive power services;
>
> judj—vector of judicial power services.

Addition of a, b, C—vectors makes it possible to obtain aggregate R—vector, which makes can be recorded as:

$$R = \pm \text{leg} \pm \text{exei} \pm \text{judj}$$

The expenditure part of all these three processes enables us to asses that created specific services of legislative, executive and judicial character represent economic product appearing in a services form.[1]

1. If volume of judicial power services is noticeably exceeding the services of legislative and executive powers, graphically it can be shown in the following parallelepiped shape:

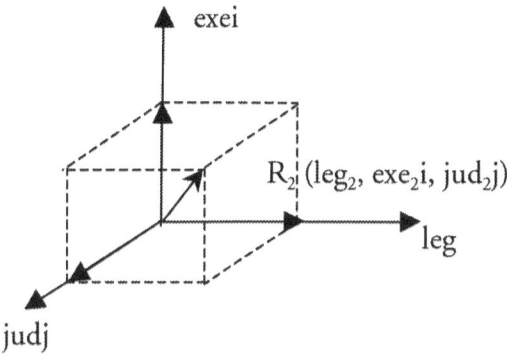

In the above option the «parallelepiped of state power services» is stretched towards the judicial branch of power.

2. If volume of executive power services is largely exceeding the services of legislative and judicial power, vector b1i will have its maximum value, as shown graphically:

---

[1] The direction of the aggregate vector R, i.e. of the state structure vector, is changeable depending on the values of a, b, C—vectors.

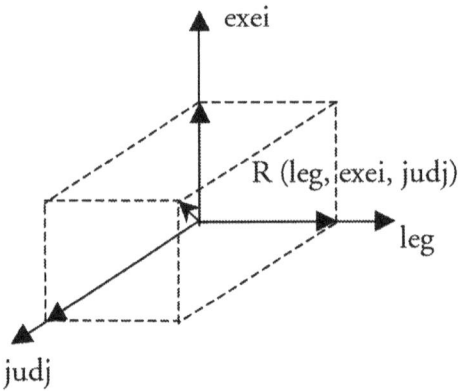

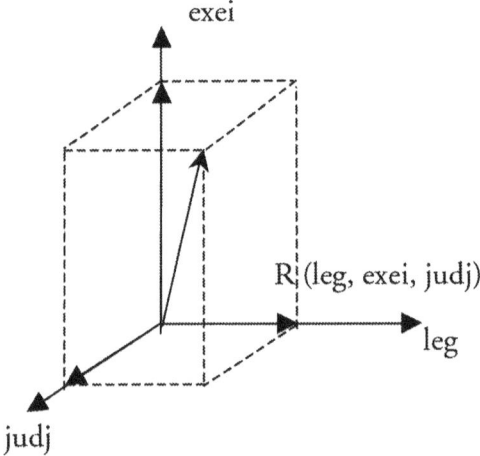

While constructing the «parallelepipeds of state power services» we shall proceed from the assumption that vectors a, b, C can take not only positive but negative estimates as well.

The services of the branches of state power are created in a socially organized structure, capable of creating specific space of legal relations. For this reason they come out as economic products. Apart from that, the expenditure of each branch of state power enables us to assess that they appear in the form of economic products. The services of the branches of state power «embrace» each citizen.

A) The Services of the Legislative Branch of Power

These services are orientated upon amendment of the laws for each of the main branches of power. I suggest that the legislative services should be represented in f three-dimensional space as follows:

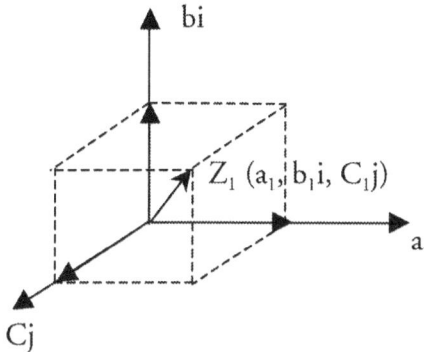

where

a₁—vector of the legislative power services is oriented on amending the laws of the legislature (for its own benefit);

b₁i—vector of the legislative power services is directed toward the improvement of the technology of creating executive power services;

C₁j—vector of the legislative power services is aimed at reforming the technology of creating judicial services.

The aggregate vector of the legislative power will be transcribed as:

$$Z_{leg} = a_1 + b_1i + C_1j$$

where

i, j—imaginary units reflecting the versatile character of state power services

B) Services of the Executive Branch of Power

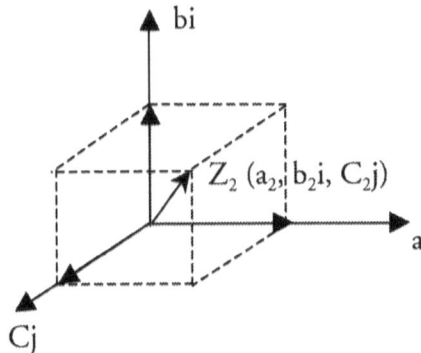

where

a₂—the vector of the past labor expenses of creating executive power services;

b₂i—the vector of the direct labor expenses of creating executive power services;

C₂j—the vector of the subject of labor of the executive branch of power.

The aggregate vector of the executive power services will be interpreted as follows:

$$Z_{exe} = a_2 + b_2i + C_2j$$

C) Services of the Judicial Branch of Power

In a three-dimensional space the services of the judicial power can be represented as:

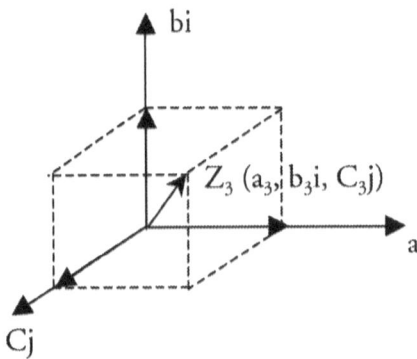

where

a₃—vector of the past labor expenses of creating judicial power services;

b₃i—vector of the direct labor expenses of creating judicial power services;

C₃j—vector of the subject of labor of the judicial branch of power.

$$Z_{jud} = a_3 + b_3i + C_3j$$

The services of the three branches of power exist in the economic space which has the following structure:

Process		Process		Process		Process	
Production	—	Distribution	—	Exchange	—	Consumption	
P Zleg P Zexe P Zjud		D Zleg D Zexe D Zjud		E Zleg E Zexe E Zjud		C Zleg C Zexe C Zjud	

CHAPTER 2

The Autocracy Index

Democracy can be "wide", can be "narrow". It is a new terms that should be worked out well. We should not confuse the concepts of the "power branch" and the "corridor branch". These are two different "things". One thing is for sure, and that is, that the ordinary citizen moves along "The Corridor of Democracy".

Many of the problems of Democracy are not spoken of. The total pre-illustration of mail, eavesdropping on telephone conversations, SMS messages, e-mails, and so on. These anti-Democractical actions are considered, by government employees, as something natural. All this is presented by the mass media as something positive, necessary for each and every one of us.

On 5th June 2005, Alexander Solzhenitsyn made an appearance on the telechannel "Russia". In his message he examined the problems of Democracy. The basic idea consisted of the following: "if in the government, there is no democracy, then you cannot seize it".

The mass media did not comment on his expressed views. The employees of the mass media kept silent. They not expect such a an open discussion.

I have some questions for Solzhenitsyn: why did he not examine the problems of Democracy in the sections of God's Ten Commandments?

If he divided the problems of Democracy in ten components, then his speech would be more convincing.

Can we take "Democracy" away from the people?

An interesting question.

Firstly, it is necessary to establish marked events, confirming that in a society, there are elements of democracy.

Secondly, every state has its specific periods of development. I would rather not compare them with the lunar phases but we can speak of certain involuntary recurrences, of the existence of the so called sinusoids of movement of the state power sphere, which will be examined in the subsequent chapters.

Today we are reminded that we are confidently walking towards autocracy.[2]

For such statements, we need strong arguments, economic estimations of autocracy and the indexes of autocracy.

What is the essence of autocracy?

It comes when there is "editing" (grooming) of the core of the basic power branches and when we simplify the basic functions of the state. One can say that "Autocracy" begins immediately after the "sterilisation" of the basic power branches. These power branches exist, but their functions are carried out by other institutions. For example, the police, in such a variant, the population falls into a society called autocracy.

In this subject there are many subjective elements, which do not allow us to say precisely where society is organized based on complete democratic principles and where the level of democracy does not exceed 10%.

Using percentages in estimating the organization of society (based on democratic principles), propels the readers to ask the following question: is it possible to "dilute" democracy up to 40%?

This question is interesting. Everything depends, on one hand, on the experimenter and, on the other hand, on the opposition of the people.

"We have to realize where there is democracy, where there is autocracy, where there is «miracle-working Democracy». In the first, second and third cases, estimations are necessary. Today they are missing. There is no unit of measurement for democracy. There is no complex index of democracy. There are no estimations of the index of autocracy.

B) Classification of States, Depending on the Extent of Development of the Basic Three Brances of Power

Every state has its own economic space. The quality of it is dependent upon the laws fixed in the Constitution of the nation as well as the services of the Executive and Judicial branch of state power. Three vectors of state power

---

[2]   It is good, that we are not standing in one place and that we are moving.
There is a lot of discussion concerning the problems of Democracy.

make up particular space, called a legal space which can have positive and negative values of the main vectors of power: A—legislative, B—executive, C—judicial power.[3]

If the services of the executive and judicial powers reside within the framework outlined by the law, that will represent a specific option of economic space.

If executive and judicial services remain beyond the frames delineated by the law, the economic space will be of another quality, some parts of it cut out, other parts, relentlessly torn up. In some areas it will remind a patch-work quilt.

Take for instance Ethiopia, Mozambique, Angola, Afghanistan etc.

If we follow the class logic laid into the Marx's theory, we can find that:

- states may be bourgeoisie—such states are functioning within bourgeois economic space:

- states may have proletarian set up—these have proletarian economic space.

In the 21-st century we ought to refuse those state classification criteria which count over 100 years. A question arouses: Why does the classification of the states take place on the basis of criteria, which have no direct relationship to this sphere? Functional criteria reflecting the basic types of state activity: legislative, executive, judicial, must be used in the classification of the states.

Three basic functions of power = three criteria—Criteria A, Criteria B, Criteria C.

It is necessary to introduce new ones that would enable us to regard states as economic legal systems.

I suggest we use the Decarts system of coordinates.

There are only eight quadrants in three-dimensional space, not more than that (see pic. 2).

---

[3]   Three basic functions of state power should correspond to the three criteria used in classification of states.

And why not classify those 200 states judging by the primary functions endowed their authorities?

Quadrant 1:

Pic.1 represents the case when all the three branches of power are developed in the state. They function smoothly and are independent from each other.

The complex vector «R» will occur in the first quadrant, indicating:

- vector (+ leg)—the positive economic estimations of the legislative power services;
- vector (+ exei)—the positive economic estimations of the executive power services;
- vector (+ judj)—the positive economic estimations of the judicial power services.

This is the option when all the above services have a positive effect on the economy of this sphere.

The total vector $R_1 = +$ leg + exei + judj

In quadrant 2:

- vector (+ leg)—the positive economic estimations of the legislative power services;
- vector (- exei)—the negative economic estimations of the executive power services;
- vector (+ judj)—the positive economic estimations of the judicial power services.

This is the case when executive power exceeds its authority.

The total vector $R_2 = +$ leg - exei + judj

In quadrant 3:

- vector (- leg)—the negative economic estimations of the legislative power services;
- vector (- exei)—the negative economic estimations of the executive power services;
- vector (+ judj)—the positive economic estimations of the judicial power services.

This occurs when the services of the executive power do not facilitate the development of the state as well.

The total vector R_3 = - leg - exei + judj

In quadrant 4:

- vector (- leg)—the negative economic estimations of the legislative power services;
- vector (+ exei)—the positive economic estimations of the executive power services;
- vector (+ judj)—the positive economic estimations of the judicial power services.

This will happen when legislative power services impede the development of the state.

The total vector R_4 = - leg + exei + judj

In quadrant 5:

- vector (- leg)—the negative economic estimations of the legislative power services;
- vector (+ exei)—the positive economic estimations of the executive power services;
- vector (- judj)—the negative economic estimations of the judicial power services.

In this case, legislative power services do not contribute to the development of the state sphere and judicial power is corrupt. It has no institution of jury etc.

The total vector R_5 = - leg + exei - judj

In quadrant 6:

- vector (+ leg)—the positive economic estimations of the legislative power services;
- vector (+ exei)—the positive economic estimations of the executive power services;
- vector (- judj)—the negative economic estimations of the judicial power services.

The total vector R_6 = + leg + exei - judj

This is the case when legislative power services do not stimulate the development of the society and the judicial power performs without the institution of jury.

In other words, it is the case when the juridical power performs the functions of military tribunals.

Quadrant 7.

If a state has a functioning legislative power, though the remaining two branches create services with a negative sign. In accordance with the suggested classification, the complex vector R will be placed in quadrant 7:

- vector (+ leg)—the positive economic estimations of the legislative power services;

- vector (- exei)—the negative economic estimations of the executive power services;

- vector (- judj)—the negative economic estimations of the judicial power services.

The total vector R_7 = + leg - exei - judj

Quadrant 8.

In case all the three branches of power are badly developed, in line with the above classification, the place of the state sphere will be found in quadrant 8:

- vector (- leg)—the negative economic estimations of the legislative power services;

- vector (- exei)—the negative economic estimations of the executive power services;

- vector (- judj)—the negative economic estimations of the judicial power services.

The total vector R_8 = - leg - exei - judj

The use of the Cartesian system of coordinates as well as the vector approach makes it possible to perform classification of countries depending on the extent of development of all the three branches of power.

Table of Estimates of the Three Branches of Power

Number of quadrant	Estimations of vectors a, b, c		
	№ 1	№ 2	№ 3
1. Quadrant № 1	$+ leg_1$	$+ exe_1i$	$+ jud_1j$
2. Quadrant № 2	$+ leg_1$	$- exe_1i$	$+ jud_1j$
3. Quadrant № 3	$- leg_1$	$- exe_1i$	$+ jud_1j$
4. Quadrant № 4	$- leg_1$	$+ exe_1i$	$+ jud_1j$
5. Quadrant № 5	$- leg_1$	$+ exe_1i$	$- jud_1j$
6. Quadrant № 6	$+ leg_1$	$+ exe_1i$	$- jud_1j$
7. Quadrant № 7	$+ leg_1$	$- exe_1i$	$- jud_1j$
8. Quadrant № 8	$- leg_1$	$- exe_1i$	$- jud_1j$

I suggest to consider the economic side of Democracy.

At the first stage it is necessary to sort out the resources entering the state power sphere.

At the second stage, we must economically estimate each of these resources.

CHAPTER 3

The Economic Arithmetics of the State Power

A) The Power Services in a Democratic Society

Let us begin with fact that the services of the three power branches have qualitative distinctions: the services of executive power differ from the services of the judicial power branch and from the services of the legislative power branch. The services of the three power branches are of different quality. This circumstance is the basis for the independent arrangement of the meaning of these services in a Cartesian system of coordinates.

How can we carry out the general calculation of the power services?

What estimations of the power branches we can arrange on the coordinates X, Y, Z.

The first estimates, which we should use before solving the problems of the state power sphere, are the expenses on each of the power branches. The expenses related to the creation of the boons and services have always represented a part of the cost of the created economic product. In our case, the Economic products are the services of the legislative, executive and judicial power branches.

Product—p_1

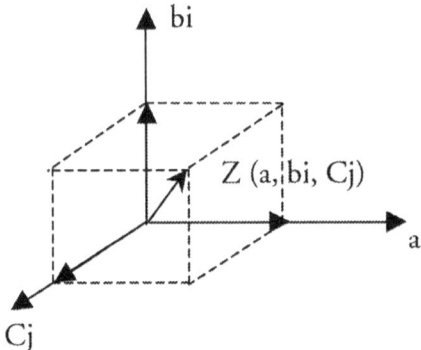

where

a—the estimates of the expenses of the legislative power branch

bj—the estimates of the expenses of the executive power branch

cj—the estimates of the expenses of the judicial power branch

The services of the power sphere are of different quality, but they can make exchanges amongst themselves of certain proportions on the basis of an expense attribute.

We can be advised to take advantaged by the tried method: the "expenses-production", which has been applied for several long years in central economic institutes. It was widely uses by the Nobel Price Winner Vassily Leontief.

This method was valid in the 20th Century.

Today, in the 21st Century this method should be considerably expanded, as well as changed.

I am going to consider the expenses of power branches in a section of four economic relations:

-    Production relations—p

-    Distribution relations—d

-    Exchange relations—e

-    Consumption relations—c

The use of the four kinds of economic relations has allowed us to make the following logical table.

Process of production	Process of distribution	Process of exchange	Process of consumption
Expenses related to the movement of product—p_1	Expenses related to the movement of product—d_1	Expenses related to the movement of product—e_1	Expenses related to the movement of product—c_1
The estimates of the expenses of the legislative power branch—p_2	The estimates of the expenses of the legislative power branch—d_2	The estimates of the expenses of the legislative power branch—e_2	The estimates of the expenses of the legislative power branch—c_2
The estimates of the expenses of the executive power branch—p_3	The estimates of the expenses of the executive power branch—d_3	The estimates of the expenses of the executive power branch—e_3	The estimates of the expenses of the executive power branch—c_3
The estimates of the expenses of the judicial power branch—p_4	The estimates of the expenses of the judicial power branch—d_4	The estimates of the expenses of the judicial power branch—e_4	The estimates of the expenses of the judicial power branch—c_4
Index—p	Index—d	Index—e	Index—c

The table reflects the expense part of the movement of the services of the three basic power branches in economic space.[4]

This table has allowed us to systematize the expenses, which are related to the movement of the three power branches in economic space, in the sections of the four kinds of economic relations.

---

[4]   Which estimates of the power branch can we arrange in the coordinates X, Y, Z.
To estimate of the activity of the "Headquarters of the Democracy", we have to invent something new.

This table has allowed us to present "The Democratic Atmosphere" in a compact view consisting of the services of the three power branches, but with estimations reflecting the expenses part of this "Atmosphere".

Index $P = P1 + P2i + P2j$—expenses related to the production of the services of the three power branches

Index $D = D1 + D2i + D2j$—expenses related to the distribution of the services of the three power branches

Index $E = E1 + E2i + E2j$—expenses related to the exchange of the services of the three power branches

Index $C = Ci + C2i + C2j$—expenses related to the consumption of the services of the three power branches

In each country the structure of the expenses of the creation of the "National Atmosphere of Democracy" has its own features.

<u>Next Stage</u>

I suggest examining the logical side of the estimations of state power, reflecting the productive activity of its branches, within the framework of economic relations:

p—production

d—distribution

e—exchange

c—consumption

At first glance, the system of estimations can be represented as such[5]

The table reflecting the resultative side of the movement of the services of the three basic power branches in economic space.

---

[5]   We have to keep in mind that the services of the three power branches are quantitatively incommensurable, but they are homogeneous in their expenses attribute.

Process of production	Process of distribution	Process of exchange	Process of consumption
Results related to the movement of product—pp_1	Results related to the movement of product—dd_1	Results related to the movement of product—ee_1	Results related to the movement of product—cc_1
The economic estimates of the results of the legislative power branch—pp_2	The economic estimates of the results of the legislative power branch—dd_2	The economic estimates of the results of the legislative power branch—ee_2	The economic estimates of the results of the legislative power branch—cc_2
The economic estimates of the results of the executive power branch—pp_3	The economic estimates of the results of the executive power branch—dd_3	The economic estimates of the results of the executive power branch—ee_3	The economic estimates of the results of the executive power branch—cc_3
The economic estimates of the results of the judicial power branch—pp_4	The economic estimates of the results of the judicial power branch—dd_4	The economic estimates of the results of the judicial power branch—ee_4	The economic estimates of the results of the judicial power branch—cc_4
Index—p	Index—d	Index—e	Index—c

The aforementioned table has allowed us to present the "Atmosphere of Democracy" in a compact style, which is created by the services of the three basic power branches. Besides this, we have at our disposal the four groups of indexes.

Index PP = pp_1 + pp_2 + pp_3 + pp_4—the complex result related to the creation of the services of the three power branches

Index DD = dd_1 + dd_2 + dd_3 + dd_4—the complex result related to the creation of the services of the three power branches

Index EE = ee_1 + ee_2 + ee_3 + ee_4—the complex result related to the creation of the services of the three power branches

Index CC = $cc_1 + cc_2 + cc_3 + cc_4$—the complex result related to the creation of the services of the three power branches[6]

Each power branch creates their own specific services, which influence the process of the production, distribution, exchange and consumption of the power services which occur in society.

From the mass media we can find out that countries with a population of a hundred million people, have a low Democracy level whereas in smaller countries, Democracy reached higher levels.

The mass media often informs us of the leftist parties who come into power in Latin America, Italy, Poland and try to change the total vector of state development. In other cases a rightist party to come to power and change the inclination angle of the total power vector is reported.

All such assertions should be provided by estimates confirming the shift of the power vector to the left or to the right.

However we cannot take advantage of marine orders such as «two compass points left» or «three compass points right».

They are estimations of navigational character, and cannot help to solve the problem of defining inclination angles of the power problem.

Where does the power vector shift?

What happens with state power sphere?

The sphere of mass media is expanding its positions, challenges the «traditional» branches of state power.

As professor P. Reeves says: «The sphere of mass media has been challenging the traditional branches of power».[7]

I suggest to consider the shifting of power vector graphically as follows:

- by placing the total vector of the three basic branches of power «R_1» on axis «X»;

- by placing the total vector of the mass media «R_2» on axis «Y».

---

[6]   This indices reflect the formal side of the "Atmosphere of Democracy", which exists in the country.

[7]   «For the past 30 years now the state power has been shifting itself towards mass media».

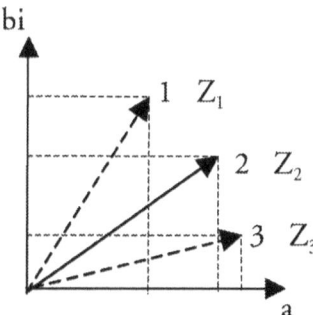

The position of the vector indicates that there has been a shift of power towards the mass media.

The position of the vector testifies to the equality between the total mass media vector Z_1 and vector of the three main branches of power Z_2.

The position of the vector Z_3 proves that the shift occurred towards the three branches of power. We shall investigate this problem at a greater length.

CHAPTER 4

The Economic Arithmetics in the Mass Media Sphere

It is difficult to picture the general model of a state structure without taking into consideration the press industry, radio and TV. These three components of the mass media are of utmost importance for the life of society and state. The mass media represent a new branch of economy with inherent technology, economic relations and financial schemes.

Without the mass media present statehoods would actually resemble the democratic set-ups of some 150 years back.

The sphere of mass communication (mass information) can be interpreted at greater length provided its economic theory has been elaborated.

The lack of theory makes all deliberations on the subject vague and pointless.

The mass media sphere can be considered as being detached from the state. However, such an approach has a number of significant shortcomings:

Firstly: why consider the mass media sphere as being disconnected from the legislative power service if the former exists in the frames of the «law»?

Secondly: is it justified to investigate the mass media sphere beyond the executive power service if it is dependent on and subject to it to a certain extent?

Third: why consider the mass media sphere as being disconnected from the judicial power service?

The investigation of the mass media sphere without taking into account the services of these branches of power is a major logical mistake.

The mass media sphere develops in the framework of the state together with the services of the three branches of power.

I suggest that they be considered in the Cartesian three-dimensional system of coordinates in which the aggregate vector of the services of the above branches can be represented as follows:

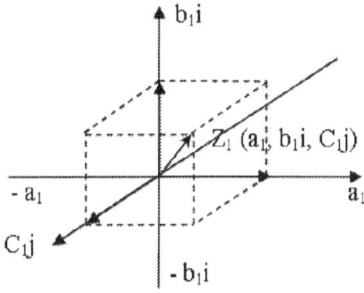

where

a_1—vector of legislative power service ($\pm$ leg);

$b_1 i$—vector of executive power service ($\pm$ exe);

$C_1 j$—vector of judicial power service ($\pm$ jud).

$$Z = \pm \text{leg} \pm \text{exe} \pm \text{jud}$$

In every state service the vectors a, bi, Cj have different values depending on the degree of development of each branch of power.

The reader will create no illusions that the movement of media values and services within economic space may happen without the services of legislative, executive and judicial power.

These three branches of power will affect any socially-organized process, including processes taking place in mass media.

Process of production, distribution, exchange and consumption of press, radio or TV services is taking place in the area of activity of the three branches of power.

All streams of resources flowing into the sphere of mass media emerge within the field of activity of legislative, executive and judicial powers:

- stream of resources entering the newspaper industry;
- stream of resources entering the fourth branch of power;

- stream of resources entering the fifth branch of power;
- stream of resources entering the sixth branch of power;
- stream of resources entering the Internet sphere.

B. Stream of resources flowing out of the newspaper, radio broadcasting and TV broadcasting industries remains under the influence of legislative, executive and judicial services.

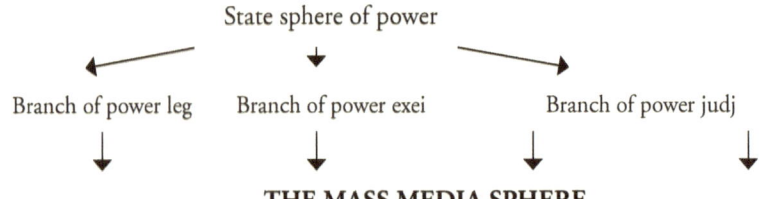

State sphere of power

Branch of power leg | Branch of power exei | Branch of power judj

THE MASS MEDIA SPHERE

Production	Distribution	Exchange	Consumption
Stream of resources entering the newspaper industry	Stream of resources entering the newspaper industry	Stream of resources entering the newspaper industry	Stream of resources entering the newspaper industry
Stream of resources entering the fourth branch of power	Stream of resources entering the fourth branch of power	Stream of resources entering the fourth branch of power	Stream of resources entering the fourth branch of power
Stream of resources entering the fifth branch of power	Stream of resources entering the fifth branch of power	Stream of resources entering the fifth branch of power	Stream of resources entering the fifth branch of power
Stream of resources entering the sixth branch of power	Stream of resources entering the sixth branch of power	Stream of resources entering the sixth branch of power	Stream of resources entering the sixth branch of power

Production	Distribution	Exchange	Consumption
Stream of resources entering the Internet sphere	Stream of resources entering the Internet sphere	Stream of resources entering the Internet sphere	Stream of resources entering the Internet sphere

There are various ways of it. Among them traditional and untraditional forms of subordination. Special laws are introduced to curb cultivation of violence, racial and other kind of hostility. In short, control over media has been carefully elaborated and is existing.

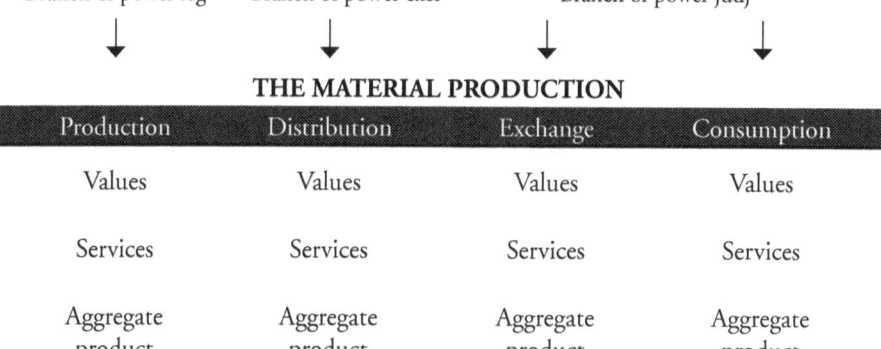

State sphere of power

Branch of power leg   Branch of power exei   Branch of power judj

THE MATERIAL PRODUCTION

Production	Distribution	Exchange	Consumption
Values	Values	Values	Values
Services	Services	Services	Services
Aggregate product	Aggregate product	Aggregate product	Aggregate product

A) Mass media reside within activity area of legislative, executive and judicial power services which can be represented as a quaternion of power services.

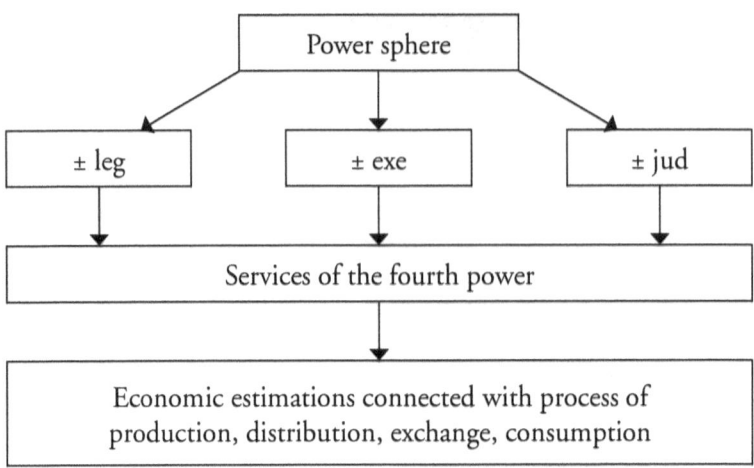

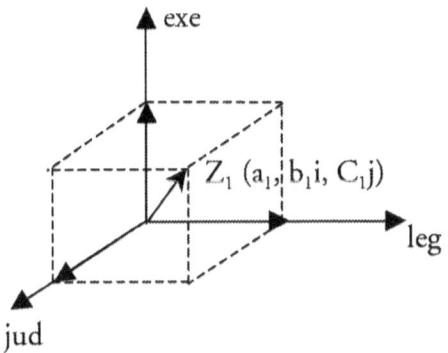

where,

   ± leg—vector of influence of legislative power services on mass media;

   ± exe—vector of influence of executive power services on mass media;

   ± jud—vector of influence of judicial power services on mass media;

These services cause shifting of all vectors of mass media development. Positive or negative signs of services of a separate branch of power reflects the character of influence on mass media.

We define inclination angles (α, β, γ) of the total vector R and what is most important we find absolute and relative qualities of this shift. It needs to be estimated.

Now we shall examine how the»quaternion of the basic branches of power» is affecting the «quaternion of mass media services».

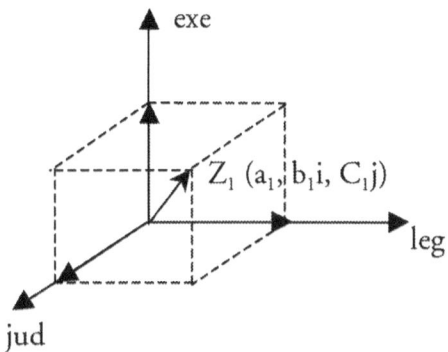

where

a—vector of newspaper industry services;

bi—vector of radio services;

Cj—vector of TV services.

Total vector of secondary branch will be recorded as follows:

$$R_2 = a_2 + b_2i + C_2j$$

Provided that the three branches of power have a certain influence on the mass media sphere, we shall add up these two parallelepipeds, i.e. two quaternions of power—«basic» and «secondary».

Another problem emerging here refer to the addition (subtraction) of «quaternion of power services» and «quaternions of secondary branches of power».

Quaternion of basic branches of power	±	Quaternion of secondary branches of power
Economic estimate of basic branches of power services (quaternion № 1)	±	Economic estimate of secondary branches of power services (TV broadcasting) (quaternion № 2)

Economic estimate of basic branches of power services (quaternion № 1)

±

Economic estimate of secondary branches of power services (Radio broadcasting) (quaternion № 3)

For the addition of quaternions № 1 and № 2 it is necessary to use operations with complex numbers.

A) The Basic Power Services and TV Broadcasting Services

The arithmetical operations of the basic power services and TV services

Economic estimate of basic branches of power services (quaternion № 1)

±

Economic estimate of secondary branches of power services (TV broadcasting) (quaternion № 2)

+
-
:
X

B) The Basic Power Services and Radio Broadcasting Services

Economic estimate of basic branches of power services (quaternion № 1)

±

Economic estimate of secondary branches of power services (Radio broadcasting) (quaternion № 2)

+
-
:
X

B. Services of Six Branches of Power in the Economic Space[8]

Services of the basic branches of power A, B, C can be investigated detachedly from the sphere of mass media. However, such an approach will hardly be proper since it is difficult to orientate oneself in the subtleties of the main branches of power without taking into consideration the minor ones. I suggest that they should be investigated as a unified block.

Block I—services of basic branches of state power—quaternion № 1.

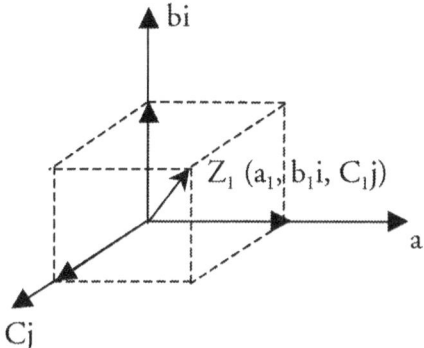

where

　　a_1—services of legislative power services;

　　b_1i—services of executive power services;

　　C_1j—services of judicial power services.

$$Z_1 = a_1 + b_1i + C_1j$$

---

[8]   Sphere of state power can be pictures as an «baobab» crown, where three main branches of power with minor branches.

Block II—services of the secondary branches of state power—quaternion № 2.

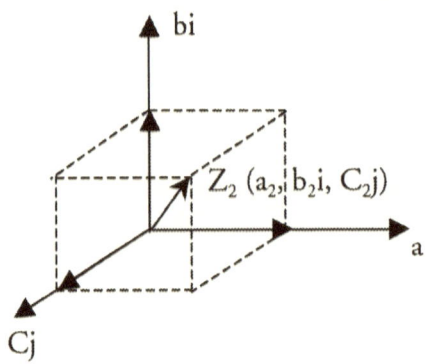

where

a$_2$—services of press industry;

b$_2$i—services of radio;

C$_2$j—services of TV.

$$Z_2 = a_2 + b_2i + C_2j$$

At this stage of examination we shall consider what is going on with the fourth, fifth and sixth branches of power like any other socially-organized process: (should avail itself of the system of estimates, criteria, indicators etc.)

The services of the 4, 5, 6 branches of power are created, distributed, exchanged and consumed.

Expenses connected with process of production	Expenses connected with process of distribution	Expenses connected with process of exchange	Expenses connected with process of consumption
Services of the fourth power Index P_4	Services of the fourth power Index D_4	Services of the fourth power Index E_4	Services of the fourth power Index C_4
Services of the fifth power Index P_5	Services of the fifth power Index D_5	Services of the fifth power Index E_5	Services of the fifth power Index C_5
Services of the sixth power Index P_6	Services of the sixth power Index D_6	Services of the sixth power Index E_6	Services of the sixth power Index C_6

Results connected with process of production	Results connected with process of distribution	Results connected with process of exchange	Results connected with process of consumption
Services of the fourth power Index P_4	Services of the fourth power Index D_4	Services of the fourth power Index E_4	Services of the fourth power Index C_4
Services of the fifth power Index P_5	Services of the fifth power Index D_5	Services of the fifth power Index E_5	Services of the fifth power Index C_5
Services of the sixth power Index P_6	Services of the sixth power Index D_6	Services of the sixth power Index E_6	Services of the sixth power Index C_6

Economic estimations connected with process of production	Economic estimations connected with process of distribution	Economic estimations connected with process of exchange	Economic estimations connected with process of consumption
Services of the fourth power Index P_4	Services of the fourth power Index D_4	Services of the fourth power Index E_4	Services of the fourth power Index C_4
Services of the fifth power Index P_5	Services of the fifth power Index D_5	Services of the fifth power Index E_5	Services of the fifth power Index C_5
Services of the sixth power Index P_6	Services of the sixth power Index D_6	Services of the sixth power Index E_6	Services of the sixth power Index C_6

Economic criteria connected with process of production	Economic criteria connected with process of distribution	Economic criteria connected with process of exchange	Economic criteria connected with process of consumption
Services of the fourth power Index P_4	Services of the fourth power Index D_4	Services of the fourth power Index E_4	Services of the fourth power Index C_4
Services of the fifth power Index P_5	Services of the fifth power Index D_5	Services of the fifth power Index E_5	Services of the fifth power Index C_5
Services of the sixth power Index P_6	Services of the sixth power Index D_6	Services of the sixth power Index E_6	Services of the sixth power Index C_6

Economic expenses of process of production	Economic expenses of process of distribution	Economic expenses of process of exchange	Economic expenses of process of consumption
Services of the fourth power Index P_4	Services of the fourth power Index D_4	Services of the fourth power Index E_4	Services of the fourth power Index C_4
Services of the fifth power Index P_5	Services of the fifth power Index D_5	Services of the fifth power Index E_5	Services of the fifth power Index C_5
Services of the sixth power Index P_6	Services of the sixth power Index D_6	Services of the sixth power Index E_6	Services of the sixth power Index C_6

Economic results of process of production	Economic results of process of distribution	Economic results of process of exchange	Economic results of process of consumption
Services of the fourth power Index P_4	Services of the fourth power Index D_4	Services of the fourth power Index E_4	Services of the fourth power Index C_4
Services of the fifth power Index P_5	Services of the fifth power Index D_5	Services of the fifth power Index E_5	Services of the fifth power Index C_5
Services of the sixth power Index P_6	Services of the sixth power Index D_6	Services of the sixth power Index E_6	Services of the sixth power Index C_6

Below we shall examine the process of it.[9]

---

[9]   Sphere of power can be pictured as an «baobab» crown where three main branches of power with minor branches.

Services of the 1, 2, 3, 4, 5, 6 branches of power exist in a common economic space which can be represented as follows:

Process of production	Process of distribution	Process of exchange	Process of consumption
Services of the legislative power	Services of the legislative power	Services of the legislative power	Services of the legislative power
Index P_1	Index D_1	Index E_1	Index C_1
Index P_2	Index D_2	Index E_2	Index C_2
Index P_3	Index D_3	Index E_3	Index C_3
Index P_4	Index D_4	Index E_4	Index C_4
Index P_5	Index D_5	Index E_5	Index C_5
Index P_6	Index D_6	Index E_6	Index C_6

Expenses connected with process of production	Expenses connected with process of distribution	Expenses connected with process of exchange	Expenses connected with process of consumption
Services of the legislative power P_1	Services of the legislative power D_1	Services of the legislative power E_1	Services of the legislative power C_1
Services of the executive power P_2	Services of the executive power D_2	Services of the executive power E_2	Services of the executive power C_2
Services of the judicial power P_3	Services of the judicial power D_3	Services of the judicial power E_3	Services of the judicial power C_3
Services of the 4-th power— Newspapers P_4	Services of the 4-th power— Newspapers D_4	Services of the 4-th power— Newspapers E_4	Services of the 4-th power— Newspapers C_4

Expenses connected with process of production	Expenses connected with process of distribution	Expenses connected with process of exchange	Expenses connected with process of consumption
Services of the 5-th power— Radio P_5	Services of the 5-th power— Radio D_5	Services of the 5-th power— Radio E_5	Services of the 5-th power— Radio C_5
Services of the 6-th power— TV P_6	Services of the 6-th power— TV D_6	Services of the 6-th power— TV E_6	Services of the 6-th power— TV C_6

Democracy Index $P = P_1 + P_2 + P_3 + P_4 + P_5 + P_6$

Democracy Index $D = D_1 + D_2 + D_3 + D_4 + D_5 + D_6$

Democracy Index $E = E_1 + E_2 + E_3 + E_4 + E_5 + E_6$

Democracy Index $C = C_1 + C_2 + C_3 + C_4 + C_5 + C_6$

Expenses connected with process of production	Expenses connected with process of distribution	Expenses connected with process of exchange	Expenses connected with process of consumption
Services of the legislative power PP_1	Services of the legislative power DD_1	Services of the legislative power EE_1	Services of the legislative power CC_1
Services of the executive power PP_2	Services of the executive power DD_2	Services of the executive power EE_2	Services of the executive power CC_2
Services of the judicial power PP_3	Services of the judicial power DD_3	Services of the judicial power EE_3	Services of the judicial power CC_3

Expenses connected with process of production	Expenses connected with process of distribution	Expenses connected with process of exchange	Expenses connected with process of consumption
Services of the 4-th power— Newspapers PP_4	Services of the 4-th power— Newspapers DD_4	Services of the 4-th power— Newspapers EE_4	Services of the 4-th power— Newspapers CC_4
Services of the 5-th power— Radio PP_5	Services of the 5-th power— Radio DD_5	Services of the 5-th power— Radio EE_5	Services of the 5-th power— Radio CC_5
Services of the 6-th power— TV PP_6	Services of the 6-th power— TV DD_6	Services of the 6-th power— TV EE_6	Services of the 6-th power— TV CC_6

Index Legislative Power = $PP_1 + DD_1 + EE_1 + CC_1$

Index Executive Power = $PP_2 + DD_2 + EE_2 + CC_2$

Index Judicial Power = $PP_3 + DD_3 + EE_3 + CC_3$

Index Newspapers = $PP_4 + DD_4 + EE_4 + CC_4$

Index Radio Broadcasting = $PP_5 + DD_5 + EE_5 + CC_5$

Index TV Broadcasting = $PP_6 + DD_6 + EE_6 + CC_6$

Index Internet = $PP_7 + DD_7 + EE_7 + CC_7$

Economic space will be meaningless unless it is supplemented by the legal system, i.e. without services of basic branches of power, protection of the interests of those who inhabit it at the stages of:

-   producing values and services;
-   distributing values and services;
-   exchanging values and services;
-   consuming values and services.

The above scheme has been compiled provided that …

Now we shall consider the option of a state power comprising six branches of power.

B) Complex Numbers—Quaternions

Graphically, a complex number can be interpreted as follows:

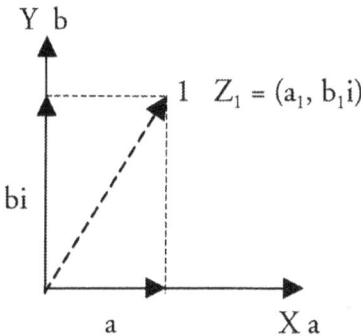

a—real number;

bi—imaginary number;

i—imaginary unity.

$Z_1 = a_1 + b_1 i$

These numbers are conveniently applied when various resources are involved, i.e. values and services:

-    material value—a;

-    immaterial value (services)—bi;

i—an imaginary unity reflecting the different nature of origin of two heterogeneous products (resources).

Complex numbers with several imaginary components are called «quaternions» by mathematicians:

$$Z = a + bi + Cj + \ldots$$

Quaternions were introduced by W. Hamilton, an Irish mathematician, in 1843. If quaternions have two imaginary components they are handy to examine in the three-dimensional system of coordinates (X, Y, Z).

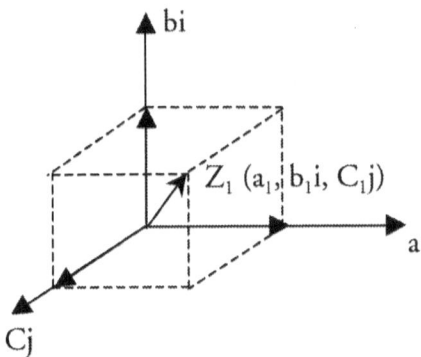

where

- vector «a» is placed on axis «X»;
- vector «bi» is placed on axis «Y»;
- vector «Cj» is placed on axis «Z».

Indices i, j, imply are heterogeneous a, b, c resources.

$$Z_1 = a_1 + b_1i + C_1j$$

Complex numbers have peculiar rules. They are different from those we are accustomed to in everyday life:

a)   addition of complex numbers;

$$z_1 + z_2 = (a_1 + b_1i) + (a_2 + b_2i) = (a_1 + a_2) + (b_1i + b_2i)$$

b)   subtraction of complex numbers;

$$z_1 - z_2 = (a_1 + b_1i) - (a_2 + b_2i) = (a_1 - a_2) + (b_1i - b_2i)$$

c)   multiplication of complex numbers;

$$z_1z_2 = (a_1 + b_1i) \times (a_2 + b_2i) = a_1a_2 + a_1b_2i + a_2b_1i + b_1b_2i^2 =$$
$$= a_1a_2 + a_1b_2i + a_2b_1i - b_1b_2 = (a_1a_2 - b_1b_2) + (a_1b_2 + a_2b_1)i$$

d)   division of complex numbers.

$$\frac{z_1}{z_2} = \frac{a_1a_2 + b_1b_2}{a_2^2 + b_2^2} + \frac{(a_2b_1 - a_1b_2)i}{a_2^2 + b_2^2}$$

Part 2

The Macroeconomy of the
Mass Media Sphere
(Double Accountancy
with Complex Numbers)

CHAPTER 1

Mass Media Traditional View

1. The Social Aim of «Tv» and «Radio Broadcasting»

According to American TV academic Mr. Nil Postman, the social aim of this branch consists of the following:

First of all, TV is a video series. We have endured a kind of evolution from printed, typographical symbols to audio-visual ones. In an average American family, TV set works usually 8 hours a day. Thus, even by nursery school age, a child has «assimilated» some 5,000 hours TV time. So, the TV today, in its own way, reflects our culture, radically different from the pervious culture based on the printed word.

- *What do we mean by «radically»?*
- *A manuscript presents the surrounding world as an idea, like an image of an object. TV information is inert. As a rule, «Daily News» is a subject for discussion, but it does not really affect our psychological state. The small screen gives us its own interpretation of the surrounding world. The events appear and disappear on it. TV-topics last 45 seconds and change with the rhythm of commercials, as a rule. Moreover, these fragments of reality are not correlated in TV, which by nature is an art of entertainment. It turns everything into «enlightenment and entertainment»; a performance, even when it pretends to be serious. Producers of such US English is spell' programs' use the logic that if you want to gather an audience, then make a enlightening and entertaining. Suppose you want to telecast on astrophysics? What is required for this? At minimum you should choose a proper and good-looking narrator, or a «star»,*

pick up some «Star Wars» videos to supplement it and so on. As a result, all is turned into «enlightenment and entertainment».

Nil Postman's view on the social aim of «TV» can be supplemented:

- firstly—the fact is that the size of the immaterial product created by «TV» and «Broadcasting» is not known
- secondly—the spare time of population catered for these branches is not considered a social aim;
- thirdly—TV and Radio services are not taken into account when calculating the standards of social well-being and other significant economic indicators.

2. The Economic Aim of «Tv» and «Radio Broadcasting

In drawing hundreds of millions of people into an intellectual service process, «TV» and «Radio Broadcasting» realize two purposes:

- **social**—i.e. mass production of «enlightenment and entertainment services» to utilize the resource of the spare time of population
- **economic**—i.e. the making of maximum profits from TV and Broadcasting.

Let's look into the matter more carefully to see how the second purpose is being realized.

In Gregory Organov's opinion, it is realized in the following manner:

«Unlike in a majority of Western countries, where TV, in one way or another is in the hands of governmental institutions, like the BBC for instance, in the US, TV has almost turned out to be under joint ownership of private and state run organizations. In practice they are unsupported by the ramified system of all-powerful commercial advertising, so in fact they sell airtime. And as soon as airtime in the US becomes the same as any other good, it brings profit in accordance to its quality. Therefore, they serve it on the American TV screen in the most rational way—«sliced» and «pre-packaged». The hardest thing to get accustomed to in the US was the method of placing American TV programs within the frames of allotted airtime.

The thing is, that these programs were cut and interrupted for quite often an indefinite time. It was a well-paid business for TV corporations, since it took account of paid ads, for which payment depended on the time and kind of placement. If it was not at «prime time», but at a less advantageous time, they paid less.

A person who is not acquainted enough with the American commerce mechanism, with its scales and methods, can hardly believe the amounts of «remuneration» for commercial ads. During one of the years under examination, the expenses of US monopolies for commercial advertising of consumer production totaled about $30 billion. The lion's share of this was spent on just TV commercials. As a matter of fact they the US mass media to «free sale» our time and frenzied profit-making, which from the principal part of future expenses on the creation of all TV shows, sports events and even information programs».[10]

The system of extracting TV profits is carried out in the following way. Let's say the NBC Company buys the rights to televise the Super Cup final from the National Football League (NFL) for $18 million. During the three-hour long transmission, the company allots 24 minutes for commercials that bring $ 31 million. If you add to this, the receipts from commercial advertisements in the course of the one-and-a-half-hour programmes preceding the Super Cup final and after its finished then you will see that the total profit is about $ 40 million. The $10 million income for NBC will be reached in the end despite taking into account the cost of the transmission itself.[11]

TV companies get such vast sums of money that they naturally spare neither strength nor resources to obtain the most popular and prestigious kind of competitions and sports events. Competitive struggle between TV companies has led to even more sudden leap in prices for TV transmissions. One can only imagine that over the last 20 years, the price for transmitting the Super Cup football final has increased 18 times!

The increase in the competitive struggle of TV companies helped sports leagues and associations increase their own profits. In the early 60's, TV and NFL profits, for example, made up 36% of their gross turnover. Now profits are counted in billions. The NFL concluded a four-year contract with TV companies two years ago to the tune of $3.6 billion. As a result, each of the 28 teams in this League receives annually $30 million. The famous, professional baseball team the New York Yankees has signed a 12-year contract with the paid channel Madison Square Garden for $500 million.

It is hard to overestimate the significance of TV in the development of the sports business in the USA. Perhaps there is no other country where interests of

---

[10]   «What is TV air?» by G. Organov.

[11]   Business World, Feb. 28, «Magazine of convenience», S. Gouskov.

these two «powers» are so closely interwoven. *«Relations between TV and sports serve as a good example of happy co-existence as they assist each other»*,—wrote famous writer J. Michner in early'70s.

Today we do not speak about survival but about sharing enormous profits. Moreover, profits from TV guarantee professional leagues a comfortable life for many years to come. In addition to that TV bosses try to own professional teams. The mergers of TV and sports businesses have taken place. Among the teams belonging to TV companies are hockey clubs such as New York Rangers, the Philadelphia Fliers; famous baseball teams, the Atlanta Braves and the California Angels, as well as the basketball club the Atlanta Hawks and others.

The relationship between professional sport and US TV can be called a «marriage of convenience».

3. The Branches of «Tv Broadcasting» and «Radio Broadcasting» as a Productive Force in Society

The solution of the economic problems faced by «TV Broadcasting» and «Radio Broadcasting» must begin by clarifying the essence of the process of interaction between the factors of this special production. The following participate in it:

- Labor resources of «TV Broadcasting» and «Radio Broadcasting» are personnel, program presenters, actors and people who possess definite professional skills and methods of «treating» TV viewers and Radio listeners during the process of intellectual servicing

- A word, a sound, a picture, etc. are instruments of labor in «TV Broadcasting» and «Radio Broadcasting»

- Individual and people are subjects of labor in «TV Broadcasting» and «Radio Broadcasting».

THE SOLITARY PRODUCTIVE FORCE OF THE BRANCHES OF «TV BROADCASTING» AND «RADIO BROADCASTING»

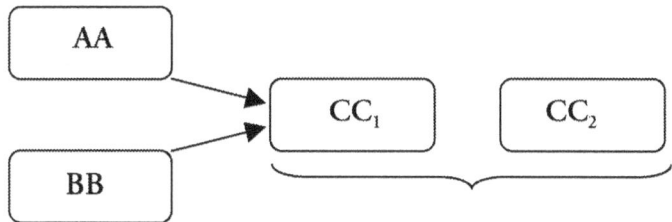

in which

> **AA**—means and instruments of «TV Broadcasting» and «Radio Broadcasting»
>
> **BB**—labor resources of «TV Broadcasting» and «Radio Broadcasting»
>
> CC_1—subject of labor—an individual
>
> CC_2—modified subject of labor—an individual
>
> **T**—time in which the interaction of the production factors creates the «enlightenment and entertainment services» of «TV Broadcasting» and «Radio Broadcasting».

The given model of «TV Broadcasting» and «Radio Broadcasting» reflects the general process that takes place in all «enlightenment and entertainment branches»: an expedient interaction between production factors, required to create «enlightenment and entertainment service». It is consumed <u>free</u>—S or for money—M.

The mode of interaction between the productive force factors of these two branches of intellectual production determines the character of production, distribution, exchange and consumption, of both the material-substantial terms of the «enlightenment and entertainment» activity and its immaterial results.

The wide application of various psychological techniques, linguistic skills, rhythmic music etc. agitate TV viewers, form the corresponding state of mind to obtain predetermined results. In short, the mass production of information services by TV with intense visual and audio effects increase the propaganda burden on the society.

The impact of TV as a means of the mass media on economic and social processes lies in its capability of intensifying current of events, in specifying and directing the trends. Judge for yourselves.

The ultimate economic purpose of TV and radio companies is to create «economic immaterial products» in the form of information or entertainment services. While consuming them you act as a spectator who has been invited to have a rest and entertain himself by watching amusing serials, musical clips etc.

Here, however, as in any self reproducing process, all expenses need to be refunded. This question still remains to be studied and settled.

There are a number of ways of payment of these services:

Option 1—budgetary funding;

Option 2—budgetary funding plus advertising;

Option 3—population and advertisers—payment for these services;

Option 4—payment for cable TV services.

I consider that TV viewers should not evade payment for the consumed specific such as TV and radio services, and put the burden of it on the advertising companies.

The situation when media services are being paid only partially is inconvenient and unsuitable from all points of view.

Every consumable resources should be paid for.

Hence:

1.   If you require a piece of information, you pay and get it.

Any other pattern proves irrelevant.

CHAPTER 2

New System of Economic Estimations in the Mass Media Sphere

When one is speaking of the mass media area of activity one will never specify the essence of it. Does this area have any boundaries?

Is it square or resembles the shape of the «Swan Lake»?

We should know the exact parameters of it.

What did it look like 20 years ago?

How large has it grown for the past several years?

Without a system of estimates it is difficult to judge whether it is expanding or shrinking.

1. Traditional Estimations of Services of Mass Media

Nowadays, the following estimates are used in the mass media: «quantity of TV viewers or radio listeners», rating of programs, etc.

These estimates, however, have been existing for decades. They do not change.

It is telling, for example, that in the sphere of economic theory of the mass media we have reached a borderline and find difficult to step over due to the lack of new approaches to the problem of estimation.

Judge it for yourselves. If such indicators as the «number of TV viewers, and radio listeners» belong to the peal of economic thinking in the mass media theory, does it mean that research into the problem of the result of media activity should be stopped?

Definitely not. There are certainly some other high points to ascend. Perhaps it is a long chain of mountains. Why not climb neighboring tops, find our own summit and move up.

Sadly, it will be the same wherever you go and whatever mount you clamber. You wall have to deal with:

-   poor provision with experienced staff;
-   inadequate funding of development projects etc.

It is necessary to indicate that there are several points of view on every existing problem. Nevertheless, you have to find the very «ridge» you are seeking, specify access routes, methods, numbers, which are to be applied to develop the necessary criteria.[12]

2. Non-Traditional Estimations of the Mass Media Services

If you deprive the people just for two or three days of the benefits provided by printed media, TV or radio you will receive specific reference points which would perfectly testify to the urgency of the media to the public.

This entailed severe consequences in the mass media showing that without information people may come to be in a kind of «time machine» taking them back to the 18-th century.

Indeed, one can hardly imagine a situation without TV or Radio highlighting state policy, current events, bringing the news to the nation. It is obvious that the lack of media may significantly complicate the life of people in the own country and elsewhere in the world.

Radio, TV and press help to settle a significant number of problems concerning the structure and functioning of a state.

Firstly, they help to develop relations among people and amend cohesion between authority and population.

Secondly, with the aid of services of printed and electronic media our spare time is being appropriated, or rather, assimilated every day.

The above media benefits have educational, enlightenment character, part of which have entertainment purposes.

---

[12]   Not long ago a serious power failure left some of the US states without electricity; a little later, a similar breakdown in Switzerland cut off electricity in Northern Italy.

For example, if direct labor expenditure comprises on an average 8 hours it takes 3-4 hours to assimilate media services every day. That implies that the daily requirement of the population in media services is 3-4 hours (on certain day even more).

In the 1940-50s the rate of the media's expansion resulted in changing the structure of the time budget of the population. People started to spend greater part of their free time resource on mass media services.

3. Cost Estimate of the Services of TV and Radio Broadcasting Companies

While evaluating the services of TV and radio corporations we shall take into account:

1. The cost of the ground TV/radio equipment including all broadcasting facilities;

2. The cost of the satellites retransmitting TV programmes;

3. Labor resource expenses;

4. Revenues obtained by TV/radio broadcasting stations.

Here again we encounter another problem. Is it necessary to include the people's spare time resource assimilated by mass media services into the cost of services provided by the TV/radio companies?

Assimilated resources of spare time exists as if hanging in the air, although it is obvious that media services are created only as a result of the assimilation of the spare time resource. Without the assimilated time resource no media services are <u>obtainable</u>.[13]

There is every reason to include ASTP in the cost of TV/radio services, since as a human resource in time value it also acts as a subject of labor and is assimilated by mass media services.

---

[13]   Monthly or yearly payment for the consumption of TV or radio services.

Here we have to point out that the A_{STP} resource is not a private property of TV and radio companies. You can insist that your spare time is your own possession and not of the neighbor living next door. He has his own spare time, it is his own personal resource.

1. Being assimilated, the working time of the population is included in the cost of the created product in accordance with the level of the workforce expenditure.

2. Drawing an analogy with the assimilated spare time as part of people's day time resource we conclude that it should be economically estimated and included in the cost of media services.

It becomes apparent that the spare time of the population is an attribute of the society irrelevant to the property of TV and radio. However, the assimilated part of the resource of media services should be incorporated in the cost of the resource along with the other resources participating in this process (as has been mentioned above, mass media resources cannot be produced without the A_{STP} resource).

To draw a parallel we shall investigate the case this problem is being tackled in the resource extracting industry.

While estimating the cost of produced oil or gas we consequently take into account the cost of the complete set of equipment installed on the surface of the earth and the part of it used for oil-well drilling under the earth plus labor force expenses.

At this point we shall draw a line for the reason that the rights of the companies producing oil and gas cease to be effective. Oil and gas reserves refer to public ownership and on this account they cannot be included in the cost of companies.

The same argument can be laid in the principle that the spare time of population resource is also a public properly. Indeed, while assimilating A_{STP} resources TV and radio companies receive weighty revenues provided that the A_{STP} resource is available. The absence of it would mean no revenues altogether.

It results from the above that natural resources such as oil, gas etc. along with the spare time of the population resource belong to the people and should remain at their disposal.

Compare the following figures. In a country with the population of 200 million people's daily spare time expenditure may come to about 1 bln. hours. Multiplied by 365 days it will make 365 billion man-hours per year. Whereas the aggregate working time comprises on an average only 500 billion man-hours.

Nevertheless, can we estimate mass media services using such an indicator as «assimilated human spare time resource»? Why not?

Doesn't there exist such an indicator as «the volume of time expenditure in the sphere of material production». Certainly. Moreover, the economic estimate of a worked out labor time comprises a definite part of the fully assessed results of labor (part labor expenses and income to be added). The same technology of calculation should be used while estimating media services.

The spare time of the population assimilated by media services appears as part of the overall assessment of the results of the media activity:

The spare time of the population resource assimilated by mass media services	$\rightarrow$	Economic estimate A_{STP}
Past labor expenses while creating mass media services	$\rightarrow$	Economic estimate C
Direct labor expenses while creating mass media services	$\rightarrow$	Economic estimate Vi
Revenues obtained for mass media services	$\rightarrow$	Economic estimate mk

The above estimates owing to their common unit of (cost) evaluation can be added to acquire a single comprehensive estimate of media services.

A_{STP} represents part of the cost of media services. It should be specially noted that the spare time of the population assimilated by media services is an independent estimate which can be used in calculations.

4. Estimation of the Spare Time of the Population

Sociological surveys show that by the age of 18 an average European spends over 20,000 hours watching TV. By 40 years the figure comes to 40,000 and by 60 it amounts to 60,000 hours.[14]

At an average it comprises 1000 hours per year.

---

[14]   By the age of 18 a European spends up to 12,000 hours for his education.
We can use our own spare time resource at our own discretion that is very remarkable in itself.

If this resource (of people's spare time) has an economic value it becomes essential to know whether it is liable to any kind of assessment or not.

The reader would obviously like to know the cost of one hour of this time.

So far these kind of researches have not been properly conducted, although some economists try to come closer to it from one side or another.

Professor A. Nilson, for example, recommends to calculate the cost of advertisement with the following assumptions:

- human resources in spare time—at 6 USD for 1000 viewers;
- given the audience is graded by the age—at 10 USD for 1000 viewers.

The main criterion used by advertisers is the popularity of TV programmes. The entire system of the TV industry depends upon this indicator and advertisement rates.

In these calculations the cost of advertisement is directly dependent on the number of viewers and the assimilated resource of the people's spare time. The more there values, the higher the price of the advertising time.

However, it would be irrelevant to maintain that an advertiser is buying the human spare time resource consumed by people while watching TV. TV and radio corporations are not actually entitled to own this most valuable human resource.

The need to investigate the reproductive economic problems of television is prompted by the difficulty of getting a clear picture of what is going on in this peculiar sphere of man's Intellectual endeavor, especially with respect to the movement of the human resources in it.

What is the essence of the aggregate TV product?

How and where do the separate parts of the aggregate TV product move?

TV is the largest segment of the intellectual sphere judging by the extent of the people's involvement in the services rendered by it. In European countries at weekends alone, TV screens attract up to 200 million people. If we complement this figure with some 150 million more people enjoying TV services on weekdays, the amount of the human resource involved can hardly be compared with any other stream of human activity. Moreover, the given figures are significantly underestimated since they do not comprise the whole Europe with East-European countries.

At present in calculations related to the TV service market, it is customary to use such an indicator as the «number of TV viewers». However, it reveals only the statistical aspect of the stream of human resource serviced by the TV and is actually contracted due to the lack of the main component—the time factor.

Proceeding from the above, I suggest the following two indicators be considered:

Indicator 1. The number of TV viewers.

Indicator 2. The number of TV viewers adjusted for the time factor.

The completeness of the second indicator as compared with the first one lies in the fact that the statistical indicator is supplemented by the time factor which transfers TV viewers on to the plane of economic estimates.

Assuming that on Saturdays and Sundays about 200 million people spend 4 hours on an average watching TV, with Indicator 2 it comes to 800 million man-hours per day.

Multiplying this quantity by 52 weeks a year we receive:

800 million man-hours X 52 Saturdays = 41,600,000,000 man-hours

800 million man-hours X 52 Sandays = 41,600,000,000 man-hours

Hence preliminary calculations reveal that on Saturdays and Sundays alone 83.2 billion man-hours are assimilated annually.

By adding the amount of spare time of the population assimilated by the TV service Monday through Friday we shall have:

150 million people X 5 days X 4 hours X 52 = 156 billion man-hours per year.

Thus, assimilation of TV services in Europe comes to:

156 billion man-hours + 83.2 billion man-hours = 239.2 billion man-hours per annum.

Being precursory, these calculations, however, can tell a lot. They obviously have to be specified taking into account the expenses connected to the assimilation of the people's spare time resource. The latter can be regarded as unconventional, but it is exactly the same human resource.

In this case it acts as a «subject of labor» and is treated as an economic resource processed by specific intellectual means of influence. On these grounds, it should be included in the cost of TV services.

And there is nothing that would contradict the elementary economic logic: TV viewers act as one of the resources absorbed by the sphere of a specific service. The resource which should cost something. It cannot be worthless.

Now, if we use a conditional unit of currency in estimating 239.2 billion man-hours, it would be worth 239.2 billion. In these estimation, we shall have to deal either with a dollar, or a euro, of course.

Thus, having estimated one hour of spare time at one euro or one USD, the resource under consideration will be worth 239.2 billion euro or USD and relevantly:

- 3 euro/hour will make up 717 billion euro;
- 5 euro/hour will come to 1 trillion 200 billion euro per annum.

To which of the following indicators in the European countries—GDP, NDP or NI—shall we add these values?

Which concrete indicator does this trillion refer to?

If to the GDP, then we shall also have to add to the above trillion expenses of the past (C) and direct (V) labor of the TV personnel.

If to the NDP, we shall add only the salaries of the TV personnel.

In relation to NI, we do not have to add any expenses of the TV stations to that same trillion.

Consequently, it is necessary to specify how the human resource in question is being assimilated.

75% of spare time European TV viewers spend on watching American programs, i.e. the bulk of the people's spare time in Europe, is assimilated by the overseas TV technologies.

Proceeding from this, 1 trillion 200 billion euro should be distributed:

- 75%, or 900 billion euro added to the US GNP;
- and only 25%, or 300 billion euro added to the US GDP of the West-European countries.

CHAPTER 3

A System of Economic Axioms in the Mass Media Sphere

For the last several years looking through newspapers and periodicals I have vainly been trying to find any article or a commentary on the issue of taxation in the mass media sphere.

How do we interpret such unanimous silence on the part of scientific research centers, taxation bodies and media representatives?

There are a number of explanations, in particular:

- absence of economic theory of the mass media;
- absence of special regulations concerning the taxation in the media sphere.

Furthermore, it can be stated that the mass media has become a source of unprecendented enrichment. In a number of countries with the ongoing process of change of forms of ownership (substitution, shift of proprietors), some entrepreneurs become millionaires in a matter of five years and multimillionaires in about ten.

Such a rapid concentration of wealth can be attributed to the following:

Firstly—a huge amount of the spare time of the population (A_{STP}) is assimilated, but in fact not included in the cost of the mass media services.

Secondly—the imperfect system of taxation in the mass media sphere, its mechanical transfer from material to the mass media sphere regardless of the peculiarities and results of activity of the latter.[15]

Taxation should be grounded on fundamental principles, axioms. The absence of such makes the entire system of it baseless.

AXIOM 1

Mass media values and service are in continuous motion in time and space and should not be observed as a static picture. Being formalized this motion can be rendered as follows:

Production	Distribution	Exchange	Consumption
Mass media values MMV	Mass media values MMV	Mass media values MMV	Mass media values MMV
Mass media services MMS	Mass media services MMS	Mass media services MMS	Mass media services MMS
The aggregate mass media product AMMP	The aggregate mass media product AMMP	The aggregate mass media product AMMP	The aggregate mass media product AMMP

At present, the provisions of Axiom 1 are not implemented in full scale since the question of the movement of mass media values and services in economic space have not been investigated in theory.

---

[15] This is for your own judgment of the mass media services (without A_{STP} resources):

$$C + V_L + m_L + S_{MM} = MMS$$

Δm—income tax;

ΔV—wage tax;

$\Delta(V + m)$—value added tax;

$\Delta(C + V + m)$—turnover tax.

In these circumstances, the system of taxation is similar to that implemented in material production.

There are no estimates, criteria or indicators revealing the character motion in the economic space of the mass media.[16]

AXIOM 2

Mass media services assimilate the human resource in their spare time. This resource is acting as a specific subject of labor with economic functions of consumption, cost, exchange etc., that is with entire economic parameters.[17]

In the process of the production of mass media services an individual—a radio listener or a TV viewer—acts in the capacity of a subject of labor.

This fact entails a problem—how and what should this specific subject of labor be related to?

Proceeding from the provisions of the classical political economy of the material sphere, the subjects of labor are referred to an expenditure part since they act as such. This is one variant of calculation of mass media services.

In case the radio and TV audience is related to the income segment we receive another variant of their calculation.

To have a clearer picture here we shall apply an analogy method.

As an example, we can investigate the situation in the resource producing the branches of economy. For instance, in the process of extracting oil and gas the production resources appear as a subject of labor, i.e. the resources produced are oil and gas.

On the other hand, the extracted energy resources come out as a result—economic value—the ultimate economic product of the oil or gas and mining industry. The produced oil and gas and coal, are assessed not as an expenditure but as a resultant part of the created product. In line with the above logic the cost of the oil and gas output will be estimated as follows:

$$C + V + Res(Oil) = EP$$

where

---

[16]   Maybe media values and services «split up» in the air into several parts? And what is the trajectory of their movement?

These questions can be answered only after we define the component parts of mass media services.

[17]   Economic estimation of mass media services with the use of complex numbers.

C—past labor expenses connected to the production of oil;

V—direct labor expenses related to the production of oil and gas;

Res—the result of the produced resource—oil and gas.

The produced resource appears as the ultimate product and by subtracting past labor expenses (V) we receive the amount of the income.

$$\text{Res} - (C + V) = \text{Income}$$

If we change in this instance the name of the resources, e.g. produced (assimilated) oil, gas, coal etc. for the resource of the spare time of the population assimilated by mass media services then, according to this formula, radio listeners and TV-viewers will constitute the income part of the item. The process of creating mass media services is accompanied by the assimilation of the spare time of radio listeners and TV-viewers. The assimilated resource appears as a result.[18]

Mass media services can be represented in the three-dimensional space:

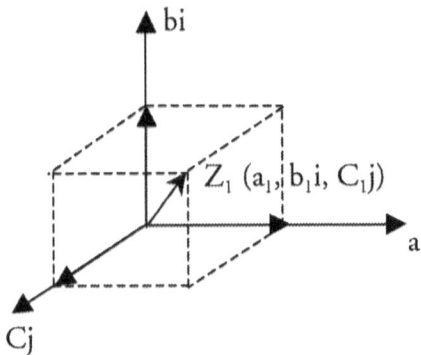

where

C—past labor expenses related to the assimilation of the people's spare time by mass media services;

---

[18]   Although in the media sphere this classical provision proves not to be effective, it is interesting to mention a commonplace phenomenon: in all three spheres—mass media, oil and gas producing industries—every high—ranking manager becomes a millionaire in about 5 years

V—direct labor expenses connected to the assimilation of the people's spare time by mass media services;

A_{STP}—spare time of the population assimilated by mass media services. A TV-viewer, or a radio listener perform as a subject of labor on the one hand, and as a specific result (as is the case with the oil, gas and coal), on the other.

The aggregate vector of media services will be displayed as follows:

$$C_{MAS} + V_{MAS} + A_{STPM} = SER_{MM}$$

$\longrightarrow$ T—the tax imposed on the spare time assimilated by media services

where

T—the tax on the human resource assimilated in the spare time (A_{STP});

SER_{MM}—economic product.

The substance of this tax is similar to the one imposed on the natural resources.

AXIOM 3

The making of media services is considered as finished as soon as a radio or a TV is switched off. The media services behave like twinkling stars. They occur only at the movement of their creation. They appear and disappear. Such is the specific character of the economic product of mass media services.

Such a non-standard circumstance will require the application of particular numbers thought to be most appropriate for unconventional situations. They are identified as imaginary and the entire class of them as complex numbers with an uncommon operational system:

a)   addition of complex numbers;

$$z_1 + z_2 = (a_1 + b_1 i) + (a_2 + b_2 i) = (a_1 + a_2) + (b_1 i + b_2 i)$$

b)   subtraction of complex numbers;

$$z_1 - z_2 = (a_1 + b_1 i) - (a_2 + b_2 i) = (a_1 - a_2) + (b_1 i - b_2 i)$$

c) multiplication of complex numbers;

$$z_1z_2 = (a_1 + b_1i) \times (a_2 + b_2i) = a_1a_2 + a_1b_2i + a_2b_1i + b_1b_2i^2 =$$
$$= a_1a_2 + a_1b_2i + a_2b_1i - b_1b_2 = (a_1a_2 - b_1b_2) + (a_1b_2 + a_2b_1)i$$

d) division of complex numbers.

$$\frac{z_1}{z_2} = \frac{a_1a_2 + b_1b_2}{a_2^2 + b_2^2} + \frac{(a_2b_1 - a_1b_2)i}{a_2^2 + b_2^2}$$

AXIOM 4[19]

While assessing taxes in the mass media sphere, real numbers with customary arithmetic operations of addition, subtraction, multiplication and division have been used so far. However, such an approach has a number of drawbacks which have a negative impact on the taxation system. You judge for yourself. Due to the fact that a variety of resources are involved in the process of production, distribution, exchange and consumption of mass media values and services it becomes necessary to use particular numbers which reflect this specificity, that is complex numbers including quaternions.

I propose to resort to them and their operational system in the economic theory of the mass media in a separate chapter concerning the taxation in the mass media sphere. There is an objective need in using complex numbers to calculate media taxes.

Thus the core of Axiom 4 is that if mass media values and services are estimated with the use of complex numbers, taxation of this field of activity will also require to use them.

We shall not refuse the group of numbers which permit the upgrade of the taxation system in this sphere.

Complex numbers should be used as broadly as possible, bearing in mind that the operations of addition, subtraction, multiplication and division with them are not similar to those we have been accustomed to.

---

[19] APPLICATION OF COMPLEX NUMBERS IN THE CALCULATION OF TAXES IN THE MASS MEDIA SPHERE

CHAPTER 4

The Mass Media as an Economic System

1. The Dual Structure of Media Sphere

I suggest that the economy of the mass media should be viewed through the prism of complex numbers.

The inward logic of a complex number consists in the following:

1. Thesis   Real numbers—a
2. Antithesis Imaginary number—bi
3. Synthesis   Complex numbers—$Z = a + bi$

Complex numbers bring in originality, create new approaches to the classification of economic categories in the mass media. With their aid the economic theory of the media sphere can develop into an ideal analytical construction from every point of view. Judge it for yourself.

If we apply the logic of a complex number, the following classification can be made:

1. Mass media values are «real values» with corresponding real numbers—a;
2. Mass media services are «imaginary values» with relevant imaginary numbers—bi;
3. The aggregate mass media product is a «complex value» with appropriate complex numbers—$Z = a + bi$;

where i—is the index revealing the different character of resources (economic products);

Mass media values are being displayed in material and immaterial (as services) forms.

The different nature of the origin of these values and services has an impact on economic relations among people as far as the production, distribution, exchange and consumption is concerned.

2. Mass Media Resources and Economic Relations

The «tools of labor», «subject of labor», «means of labor», «labor resources» refer to material elements of productive forces. A productive force appears as a system in which elements are interacting according to a definite technology.[20]

Economic relations bind together the elements of the productive forces into a single process. Only provided that there are economic relations it will be possible to create economic values and services.

The absence of economic relations will imply the lack of an economic product.

Hence, if there are relations—there is a product—there is a result.

The interrelation of the mass media elements occurs on the basis of economic relations established among people in the relevant sphere. On the one hand the connections between the «tools of labor» and «labor resources» in the spheres producing media services are maintained on a payment basis. The consumption of media services is performed free of charge, on the other hand.

The mass media sphere gives the population its services free of charge according to needs. The consumption of the mass media services occurs in the process of their creation.

Below I have outlined by dots that part of economic relations which are sold without a cost component.

---

[20]   C. INTERCONNECTION OF ECONOMIC ELEMENTS IN THE MASS MEDIA

Production process	Distribution process	Exchange process	Consumption process
Mass media values	Mass media values	Mass media values	Mass media values
Mass media services	Mass media services	Mass media services	Mass media services
The mass media aggregate product	The mass media aggregate product	The mass media aggregate product	The mass media aggregate product

3. Social Form of Relationship of Mass Media Services

Mass media services do not fall out of the production process. From the very beginning of the process they directly become a substance of a social product. It is such a form of relation in which the activity of every working person becomes socially beneficial. The above services are consumed directly bypassing the stage of exchange. The services being free for an individual do not, however, imply their costless production and distribution for the society.

By providing free services, the mass media moves apart the limits of social relations reducing at the same time the influence of commodity-money relations.

Cost and direct social relations are contrary to one another by nature. Though interopposed, they are inter complementary i.e. related to each other and forming common economic ties.

ECONOMIC RELATIONS IN THE NASS MEDIA SPHERE
MASS MEDIA VALUES

Thesis	Cost (money) form of relations in the process of producing mass media values
Antithesis	Direct social (free) form of relations in the process of producing mass media values
Synthesis	Aggregate economic relations of the mass media

MASS MEDIA SERVICES

Thesis   Cost (money) form of relations in the process of producing mass media services

Antithesis   Direct social (free) form of the relations in the process of producing mass media services

Synthesis   Aggregate economic relations of the mass media

MASS MEDIA AGGREGATE PRODUCT

Thesis   Cost (money) form of relations in the process of producing the mass media aggregate product

Antithesis   Direct social (free) form of relations in the process of producing the mass media aggregate product

Synthesis   Aggregate economic relations of the mass media aggregate product

In the table below that part of economic relations which act in combination (cost and direct social relations) has been outlined by dots.

Production	Distribution	Exchange	Consumption
Mass media values	Mass media values	Mass media values	Mass media values
Mass media services	Mass media services	Mass media services	Mass media services
The mass media aggregate product	The mass media aggregate product	The mass media aggregate product	The mass media aggregate product

4. Alignment of the Level of Development of the Media Productive Forces and Standards of Economic Relations

One of the main problems of the mass media sphere consists of the interaction of the productive forces elements and economic relations. There are certain confusions which impede the movement of the mass media economic values and services.

Option 1.

$$\left|\begin{array}{c}\text{Level of development of mass}\\\text{media productive forces}\end{array}\right|\equiv^{20}\left|\begin{array}{c}\text{Standard of economic relations}\end{array}\right|$$

Option 2.

$$\left|\begin{array}{c}\text{Level of development of mass}\\\text{media productive forces}\end{array}\right|>\left|\begin{array}{c}\text{Standard of economic relations}\end{array}\right|$$

Option 3.

$$\left|\begin{array}{c}\text{Level of development of mass}\\\text{media productive forces}\end{array}\right|<\left|\begin{array}{c}\text{Standard of economic relations}\end{array}\right|$$

Economic relations set up in the media sphere either correspond or not conform to the level of development of media productive forces.

Existing discrepancies restrain the development of mass media productive forces.

A_1

$$\left|\begin{array}{c}\text{Level of development of}\\\text{producing mass media values}\end{array}\right|\equiv\left|\begin{array}{c}\text{Standard of distributive}\\\text{relations}\end{array}\right|$$

B_1

$$\left|\begin{array}{c}\text{Level of development of}\\\text{producing mass media values}\end{array}\right|>\left|\begin{array}{c}\text{Standard of exchange relations}\end{array}\right|$$

C_1

$$\left|\begin{array}{c}\text{Level of development of}\\\text{producing mass media values}\end{array}\right|<\left|\begin{array}{c}\text{Standard of consumption}\\\text{relations}\end{array}\right|$$

---

[21] $\equiv$ - identical

A_2

$$\left| \begin{array}{c} \text{Level of development of} \\ \text{producing mass media services} \end{array} \right| \equiv \left| \begin{array}{c} \text{Standard of distributive} \\ \text{relations} \end{array} \right|$$

B_2

$$\left| \begin{array}{c} \text{Level of development of} \\ \text{producing mass media services} \end{array} \right| > \left| \text{Standard of exchange relations} \right|$$

C_2

$$\left| \begin{array}{c} \text{Level of development of} \\ \text{producing mass media services} \end{array} \right| < \left| \begin{array}{c} \text{Standard of consumption} \\ \text{relations} \end{array} \right|$$

CHAPTER 5

Periodic Table of Economic Relations Connected with the Movement of Mass Media Values and Services in the Economic Space

I suggest that the economy of the mass media should be viewed through the prism of complex numbers.

The inward logic of a complex number consists in the following:

1. Thesis   Real numbers—a
2. Antithesis   Imaginary number—bi
3. Synthesis   Complex numbers—$Z = a + bi$

Complex number bring in originality, create new approaches to the classification of economic categories in the mass media. With their aid the economic theory of the media sphere can develop into an ideal analytical construction from every point of view. Judge it for yourself.

If we apply the logic of a complex number the following classification can be made:

1. Mass media values are «real values» with corresponding real numbers—a;
2. Mass media services are «imaginary values» with relevant imaginary numbers—bi;
3. The aggregate mass media product is a «complex value» with appropriate complex numbers—$Z = a + bi$;

where i—is the index revealing different character of resources (economic products);

Mass media values are being displayed in material and immaterial (as services) forms.

The different nature of the origin of these values and services has an impact on economic relations among people as far as the production, distribution, exchange and consumption is concerned.

The opposed—material and immaterial—origin of mass media values and services, as I have pointed out, will necessitate the usage of complex numbers.

Complex number require particular treatment since we deal with specific arithmetic, attribute operational system of:

A)—addition

B)—subtraction

C)—multiplication

D)—division

You simultaneously add, subtract, multiply and divide real and imaginary numbers without violating any of the rules.

There is another point to be mentioned: our decisions will be sought in the bounds of complex numbers provided they are being used. And adversely, being neglected, the conclusion will remain in the framework outlined by real numbers. In this case part of the necessary decisions will not be made.

1. Classification of Economic Relations Connected with the Movement of Mass Media Values And Services

1. Economic relations of the «production» connected to the movement of MM values and services.

In general, the above can be recorded as follows:

1. Thesis   Economic relations of «production» connected to the MM values—«a»

2. Antithesis   Economic relations of «production» connected to the MM services—«bi»

3. Synthesis   Economic relations of «production» connected to the complex MM product $Z = a + bi$

This can also be shown graphically as:

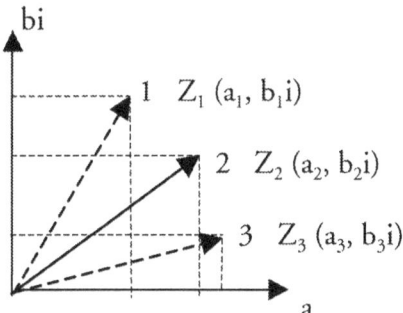

The graph reveals the following:

If vector Z is in position 1, then in the frames of the relations of the «production» relations connected to the MM services prevail.

If vector Z occupies position 2 coinciding with the bisector of the angle, then the economic relations of the «production» connected to the MM values and services are 50/50.

If the vector Z is in position 3, then in the frames of the relations of the production relations connected to the MM values are prevalent.

2. Economic relations of «distribution» connected to the movement of MM values and services.

In general the above can be recorded as follows:

1. Thesis   Economic relations of the «distribution» connected to the MM values—«a»

2. Antithesis   Economic relations of the «distribution» connected to the MM services—«bi»

3. Synthesis   Economic relations of the «distribution» connected to the complex MM product Z = a + bi

This can also be shown graphically as:

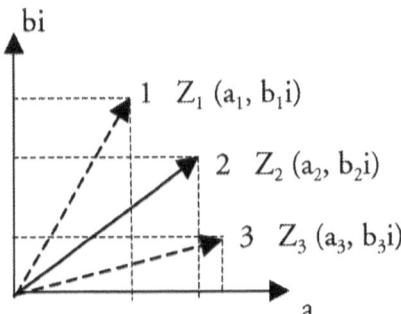

The graph reveals the following:

If vector Z is in position 1, then in the frames of the relations of the «distribution» relations connected to the MM services prevail.

If vector Z occupies position 2 coinciding with the bisector of the angle, then the economic the relations of the «distribution» connected to the MM values and services are 50/50.

If the vector Z is in position 3, then in the frames of the relations of the distribution relations connected to the MM values are prevalent.

3. Economic relations of the «exchange» connected to the movement of MM values and services.

In general the above can be recorded as follows:

1. Thesis   Economic relations of the «exchange» connected to the MM values—«a»

2. Antithesis Economic relations of the «exchange» connected to the MM services—«bi»

3. Synthesis   Economic relations of the «exchange» connected to the complex MM product $Z = a + bi$

This can also be shown graphically as:

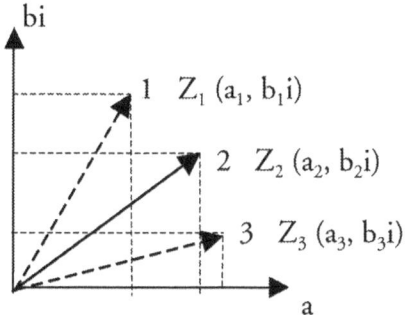

The graph reveals the following:

If vector Z is in position 1, then in the frames of the relations of the «exchange» relations connected to the MM services prevail.

If vector Z occupies position 2 coinciding with the bisector of the angle, then the economic the relations of the «exchange» connected to the MM values and services are 50/50.

If the vector Z is in position 3, then in the frames of the relations of the exchange relations connected to the MM values are prevalent.

4. Economic relations of the «consumption» connected to the movement of MM values and services.

In general the above can be recorded as follows:

1. Thesis   Economic relations of the «consumption» connected to the MM values—«a»

2. Antithesis   Economic relations of the «consumption» connected to the MM services—«bi»

3. Synthesis   Economic relations of the «consumption» connected to the complex MM product $Z = a + bi$

This can also be shown graphically as:

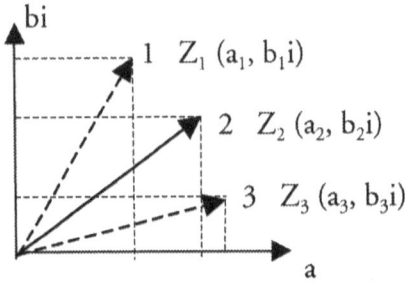

The graph reveals the following:

If vector Z is in position 1, then in the frames of the relations of the «consumption» relations connected to the MM services prevail.

If vector Z occupies position 2 coinciding with the bisector of the angle, then the economic relations of the «consumption» connected to the MM values and services are 50/50.

If the vector Z is in position 3, then in the frames of the relations of the consumption relations connected to the MM values are prevalent.

Periodic Table of Economic Relations Connected with the Movement of Mass Media Values and Services in the Economic Space

Process of production	Process of distribution	Process of exchange	Process of consumption
Mass media values	Mass media values	Mass media values	Mass media values
Mass media services	Mass media services	Mass media services	Mass media services
The mass media aggregate product	The mass media aggregate product	The mass media aggregate product	The mass media aggregate product

Calculation GDP, NDP, NI Created in the Mass Media Sphere

Today Gross Domestic Product (GDP), Net Domestic Product (NDP), Net Income (NI) and other economic indicators are calculated with the help of an expense and income method for the branches of the material sphere.

As for my research, I proceed that if there are differences between the material and intellectual sphere of production (and they do really exist), it is because there are different methods of calculating material and intellectual production. This is obvious.

Using the above criteria allows me to point out two divisions with in the mass media sphere:

1 Division: production of mass media values.

2 Division: production of mass media services.

As for as the <u>branches of Division I</u> of the mass media sphere of production are concerned, an economic structure of the product being created could be represented as such:

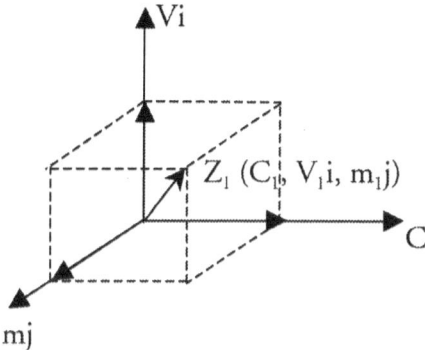

where

C_1—expenses of past labor connected with creation of mass media values;

V_1i—wages of the employees creating GDP_1;

m_1j—a profit obtained from the creation of the mass media product (GDP_1).

$$C_1 + V_1i + m_1j = GDP_1$$

As for as the <u>branches of Division II</u> of the mass media sphere of production are concerned, an economic structure of mass media service could be represented as follows:

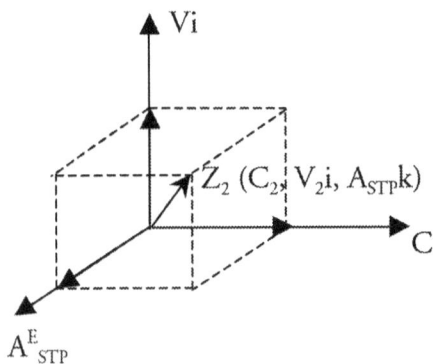

where

C_2—expenses of past labor connected with creation of mass media services;

V_2i—wages connected with the creation of mass media services;

A_{STP}—the assimilated resource of the population's spare time by Division II.

$$C_2 + V_2i + A_{STP}k = GDP_2$$

A general structure of the GDP created in mass media sphere could be represented as such:

DIALECTICAL STRUCTURE
GDP CREATED IN THE MASS MEDIA SPHERE

Thesis   GDP created in the mass media sphere of Division I

$C_1 + V_1i + m_1j = GDP_1$

Antithesis GDP created in the mass media sphere of Division II

$C_2 + V_2i + A_{STP}k = GDP_2$

Synthesis GDP created in the mass media sphere of Divisions I & II

$(C_1 + C_2) + (V_1 + V_2)i + m_1j + A_{STP}k = GDP$

DIALECTICAL STRUCTURE
OF THE NET DOMESTIC PRODUCT (NDP) CREATED IN THE MASS MEDIA SPHERE

Thesis   NDP created in the mass media sphere of Division I—

$$GDP_1 - C_1 = V_1i + m_1j$$

Antithesis   NDP created in the mass media sphere of Division II—

$$GDP_2 - C_2 = V_2i + A_{STP}k$$

Synthesis   NDP created in the mass media sphere as a whole

$$GDP_1 + GDP_2 - (C_1 + C_2) = (V_1 + V_2)i + m_1j + A_{STP}k$$

DIALECTICAL STRUCTURE
OF NET INCOME (NI) CREATED IN THE MASS MEDIA SPHERE

Thesis   NI created in the mass media sphere of Division I—

$$GDP_1 - (C_1 + V_1i) = m_1j$$

Antithesis   NI created in the mass media sphere of Division II—

$$GDP_2 - (C_2 + V_2j) = A_{STP}k$$

Synthesis   Net Income (NI) created in the mass media sphere as a whole—

$$GDP_1 + GDP_2 - (C_1 + C_2) - (V_1 + V_2)i = m_1j + A_{STP}k$$

2. Application of Complex Numbers in the Estimation of Expenses Connected to the Movement of Mass Media Values and Services

Periodic Table of Economic Relations
Connected with the Movement of
Mass Media Values and Services in the Economic Space

Process of production	Process of distribution	Process of exchange	Process of consumption
Expenses of production of mass media values VP_1	Expenses of production of mass media values VD_1	Expenses of production of mass media values VE_1	Expenses of production of mass media values VC_1

Process of production	Process of distribution	Process of exchange	Process of consumption
Expenses of production of mass media services SP_2	Expenses of production of mass media services SD_2	Expenses of production of mass media services SE_2	Expenses of production of mass media services SC_2
Expenses of production of aggregate mass media product MPP_3	Expenses of production of aggregate mass media product MPD_3	Expenses of production of aggregate mass media product MPE_3	Expenses of production of aggregate mass media product MPC_3

The aggregate economic expenses will be written as follows:

$$Z_1 = VP_1 + VD_1i + VE_1j + VC_1k$$
$$ZZ_2 = SP_2 + SD_2i + SE_2j + SC_2k$$
$$ZZZ_3 = MPP_3 + MPD_3i + MPE_3j + MPC_3k$$

, where

    i, j, k—is an imaginary unit

The matrix of mass media values and services movement can be presented as follows:

$$ZZZ = \begin{vmatrix} p_1 & d_1 & e_1j & c_1k \\ p_2 & d_2 & e_2j & c_2k \\ p_3 & d_3 & e_3j & c_3k \\ p_4 & d_4 & e_4j & c_4k \end{vmatrix}$$

3. Calculation of Expenses Connected to the «Production» of the Aggregate Mass Media Product

DIALECTICAL STRUCTURE OF LABOR EXPENSES WHILE PRODUCING MASS MEDIA VALUES AND SERVICES

A. THESIS

DIALECTICAL STRUCTURE OF LABOR EXPENSES WHILE CREATING MASS MEDIA VALUES

1. Thesis   Past labor expenses of creating mass media values—a_1
2. Antithesis   Direct labor expenses of creating mass media values—b_1i
3. Synthesis   Aggregate labor expenses (past and direct) of creating mass media values $Z_1 = a_1 + b_1i$

B. ANTITHESIS

DIALECTICAL STRUCTURE OF LABOR EXPENSES WHILE CREATING MASS MEDIA SERVICES

1. Thesis   Past labor expenses of creating mass media services—a_2
2. Antithesis   Direct labor expenses of mass media services—b_2i
3. Synthesis   Aggregate labor expenses (past and direct) of creating executive mass media services $Z_2 = a_2 + b_2i$

C. SYNTHESIS

DIALECTICAL STRUCTURE OF LABOR EXPENSES WHILE PRODUCING AGGREGATE MASS MEDIA PRODUCT

1. Thesis   Aggregate past labor expenses $(a_1 + a_2 + a_3)$ of creating the aggregate mass media product
2. Antithesis   Aggregate direct labor expenses $(b_1i + b_2i + b_3i)$ of creating the aggregate mass media product

3. Synthesis   Aggregate labor expenses (past and direct) of producing the aggregate mass media product $Z = Z_1 + Z_2 = (a_1 + a_2 + a_3) + (b_1 + b_2 + b_3)i$

4. Calculation of the Expenses Connected to the «Distribution» of the Aggregate Mass Media Product

Having examined the general aspect of the expenses connected with distribution, we shall dwell on the particulars of this problem.[22]

THESIS

DIALECTICAL STRUCTURE OF LABOR MASS MEDIA SERVICES

1. Thesis   Past labor expenses connected to the distribution of mass media values—«a_1»

2. Antithesis   Direct labor expenses connected to the distribution of mass media values—«b_1i»

3. Synthesis   Aggregate labor expenses (past and direct) connected to the distribution of mass media values—$Z_1 = a_1 + b_1i$

ANTITHESIS

DIALECTICAL STRUCTURE OF LABOR EXPENSES CONNECTED TO DISTRIBUTION OF MASS MEDIA SERVICES

1. Thesis   Past labor expenses connected to the distribution of mass media services—«a_2»

2. Antithesis   Direct labor expenses connected to the distribution of mass media services—«b_2i»

3. Synthesis   Aggregate labor expenses (past and direct) connected to the distribution of mass media services—$Z_2 = a_2 + b_2i$

---

22   It comprises the distribution of the tool of labor, the distribution of labor resources, products of labor. The character and principles of distribution depend on the legal component—right of ownership etc.

SYNTHESIS

DIALECTICAL STRUCTURE OF LABOR EXPENSES CONNECTED TO DISTRIBUTION OF AGGREGATE MASS MEDIA PRODUCT

1. Thesis   Aggregate past labor expenses $(a_1 + a_2 + a_3)$ connected to the distribution of the aggregate mass media product

2. Antithesis   Aggregate direct labor expenses $(b_1 + b_2 + b_3)i$ connected to the distribution of the aggregate mass media product

3. Synthesis   Aggregate labor expenses (past and direct) connected to the distribution of the aggregate mass media product
$$Z = Z_1 + Z_2 + Z_3 = (a_1 + a_2 + a_3) + (b_1 + b_2 + b_3)i$$

5. Calculation of Expenses Connected to the «Exchange» of the Aggregate Mass Media Product

THESIS

DIALECTICAL STRUCTURE OF LABOR EXPENSES CONNECTED TO EXCHANGE OF MASS MEDIA VALUES

1. Thesis   Past labor expenses of the exchange of mass media values—a_1

2. Antithesis   Direct labor expenses of the exchange of mass media values—$b_1 i$

3. Synthesis   Aggregate labor expenses (past and direct) of the exchange of mass media values—$Z_1 = a_1 + b_1 i$

ANTITHESIS

DIALECTICAL STRUCTURE OF LABOR EXPENSES CONNECTED TO EXCHANGE OF MASS MEDIA SERVICES

1. Thesis Past labor expenses of the exchange of mass media services—a_2

2. Antithesis Direct labor expenses of the exchange of mass media services—b_2i

3. Synthesis Aggregate labor expenses (past and direct) of the exchange of mass media services—$Z_2 = a_2 + b_2i$

SYNTHESIS

DIALECTICAL STRUCTURE OF LABOR EXPENSES WHILE EXCHANGING AGGREGATE MASS MEDIA PRODUCT

1. Thesis Aggregate past labor expenses $(a_1 + a_2 + a_3)$ while exchanging the aggregate mass media product

2. Antithesis Aggregate direct labor expenses $(b_1 + b_2 + b_3)i$ while exchanging the aggregate mass media product

3. Synthesis Aggregate labor expenses (past and direct) while exchanging the aggregate mass media product $Z = Z_1 + Z_2 + Z_3 = (a_1 + a_2 + a_3) + (b_1 + b_2 + b_3)i$

CHAPTER 6

The Mass Media in the System
of the Three Branches of State Power

1. The Three Branches of State Power

Two thousand years ago, the Romans proposed a state system comprising the legislative, executive and judicial branches of power, a model of statehood widely applied now in democratic countries. It is essential that the quality of economic space of a state is dependent upon the services of these three branches of power.

I suggest that the services of the three branches of power should be arranged in a three-dimensional space in the following way:

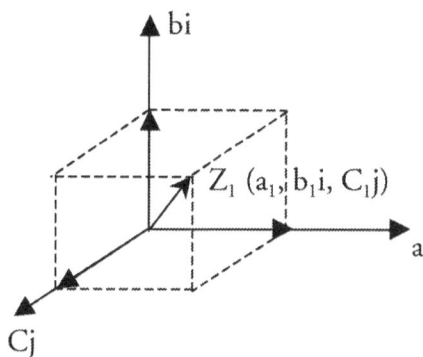

, where

- on axis X—single service vector of the legislative power (a);
- on axis Y—single service vector of the executive power (bi);
- on axis Z—single service vector of the judicial power (Cj).

The above services are being reproduced every hour, every day, every year.

The complex vector R of the three types of services can be recorded as follows:

$$R = a + bi + Cj$$

where

i, j—imaginary units reflecting versatile character of power services.[23]

The aggregate economic estimate of the services of the three branches of state power will be recorded as follows:

$$R = \pm \text{«leg»} \pm \text{«exe»} \pm \text{«jud»}$$

If the services of the three branches of power are not examined in a three dimensional space, the services of a separate branch of power overlap the services of the other branches and so forth.

This way of examination makes it difficult to comprehend what is going on in the state power sphere. The arrangement of the power vectors in the Cartesian three-dimensional system of coordinates may be considered as rewarding finding on the way of cognizing the economy of state power.

Each branch of power offers its own specific subject of labor as well as particular expenses and results.

---

[23]   Furthermore, I would also propose the inolvoduction of a new concept of a «quaternion of state power services». The substance of this new notion would reveal itself if we place:
- on axis X—the economic estimates of the legislative power services (± leg);
- on axis Y—the economic estimates of the executive power (± exe);
- on axis Z—the economic estimates of the judicial power (± jud).

A) The Services of the Legislative Branch of Power

These services are orientated upon amendment of the laws for each of the main branches of power. I suggest that the legislative services should be represented in f three-dimensional space as follows:

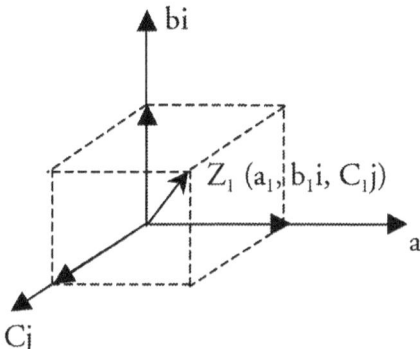

where

a_1—vector of the legislative power services is oriented on amending the laws of the legislature (for its own benefit);

b_1i—vector of the legislative power services is directed toward the improvement of the technology of creating executive power services;

C_1j—vector of the legislative power services is aimed at reforming the technology of creating judicial services.

The aggregate vector of the legislative power will be transcribed as:

$$Z_{leg} = a_1 + b_1i + C_1j$$

where

i, j—imaginary units reflecting the versatile character of state power services

B) Services of the Executive Branch of Power

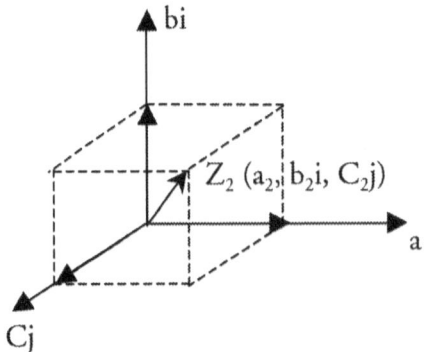

where

   a_2—the vector of the past labor expenses of creating executive power services;

   b_2i—the vector of the direct labor expenses of creating executive power services;

   C_2j—the vector of the subject of labor of the executive branch of power.

The aggregate vector of the executive power services will be interpreted as follows:

$$Z_{exe} = a_2 + b_2i + C_2j$$

C) Services of the Judicial Branch of Power

In a three-dimensional space the services of the judicial power can be represented as:

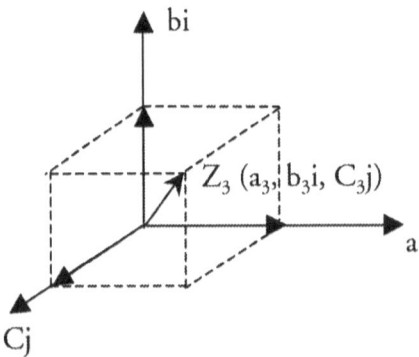

where

a₃—vector of the past labor expenses of creating judicial power services;

b₃i—vector of the direct labor expenses of creating judicial power services;

C₃j—vector of the subject of labor of the judicial branch of power.

$$Z_{jud} = a_3 + b_3i + C_3j$$

2. Influence of Three Branches of State Power Services on the Mass Media

The mass media can be considered separately from the state and state structures. However such an approach has a number of significant shortcomings:

Firstly. Why consider the mass media as being disconnected from the legislative power service if the former exists in the frames of «law»?

Secondly. Is it justifiable to investigate the mass media beyond the executive power service if it is dependent on and subject to the latter to a certain extent?

Third. Why consider the mass media as being disconnected from the judicial power service?

The investigation of the mass media without accounting for the services of these branches of power is a major logical mistake.

The mass media sphere of the society is in permanent movement. Its development occurs in the framework of the state together with the services of the three branches of power.

The mass media reside within activity area of legislative, executive and judicial power services which can be represented as a «quaternion of state power services».

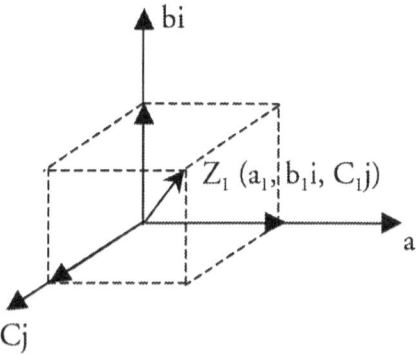

Where,

a—vector of the influence of legislative power services on the mass media ($\pm$ leg);

bi—vector of the influence of executive power services on the mass media (+ exe)—subsidiaries of mass media, (- exe)—taxes of mass media;

Cj—vector of influence of judicial power services on the mass media ($\pm$ jud);

The total vector of the three branches of power will be recorded as follows:

$$R_1 = \pm a_1 \pm b_1 i \pm C_1 j$$

or

$$R_1 = \pm \text{leg} + (\pm \text{exe})i + (\pm \text{jud})j$$

These services cause the shift of all the vectors of the mass media development. Positive or negative signs of services of a separate branch of state power reflect the character of the influence on the mass media.[24]

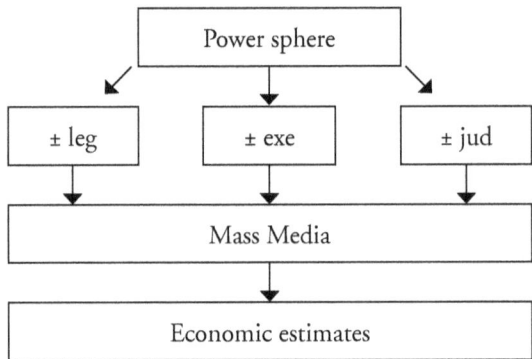

Now we shall examine how the «quaternion of the basic branches of power» is affects the «quaternion of mass media services».

---

[24]   We define the inclination angles (α, β, γ) of the total vector of state power R and what is most important we find the absolute and relative qualities of this shift.

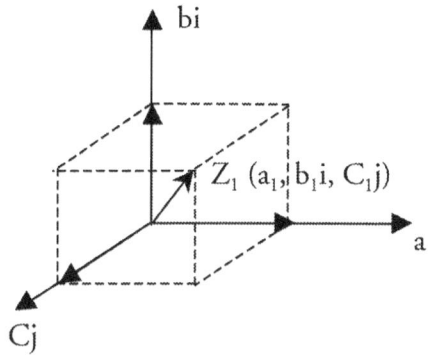

Where,

a—vector of newspaper industry services;

bi—vector of radio services;

Cj—vector of TV services.

The total vector of mass media services will be recorded as follows:

$$R_2 = a_2 + b_2 i + C_2 j$$

A) The Mass Media Sphere is Evolving Together with the Executive Power

It represents a segment of national economy and experiences all the «administrative instruments of influence» of the executive power including taxation.

(Fig. 1)

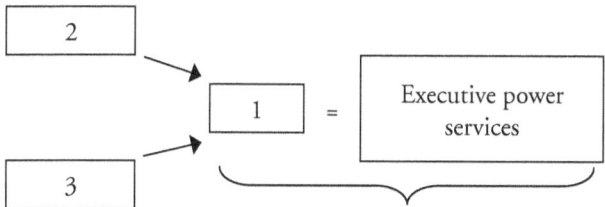

, where

1—the mass media sphere as an economic system (MMS);

2—the «administrative labor resources» of the executive power;

3—the administrative instruments of influence of the executive power including taxation;

T—the time spent on the creating the executive power service.

The interaction of the factors 1, 2, 3 (Fig. 1) results in the creation of the executive power service in time and space.

The creation of the executive power services in the mass media sphere oriented to collection of taxes can be interpreted in a broader shape as follows:

(Fig. 2)

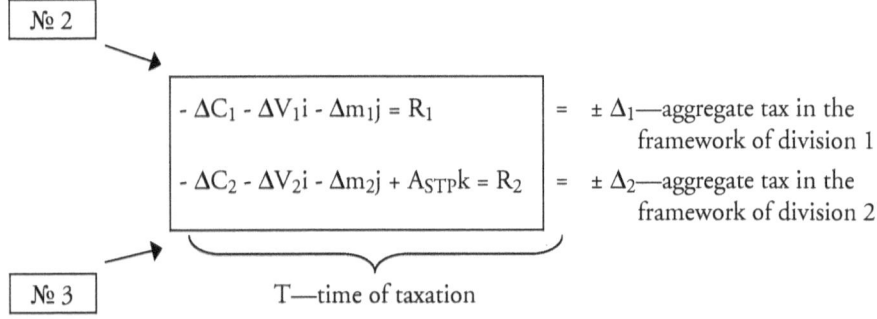

№ 2

$$- \Delta C_1 - \Delta V_1 i - \Delta m_1 j = R_1 \quad = \quad \pm \Delta_1 \text{—aggregate tax in the framework of division 1}$$

$$- \Delta C_2 - \Delta V_2 i - \Delta m_2 j + A_{STP} k = R_2 \quad = \quad \pm \Delta_2 \text{—aggregate tax in the framework of division 2}$$

№ 3   T—time of taxation

, where

$\pm \Delta_1$—tax collection in the framework of mass media division 1;

$\pm \Delta_2$—tax collection in the framework of mass media division 2;

T—time of taxation

The executive power system of services kept pace with the movement of the mass media in the economic space in some cases even surprising it. Taxation is taking place in all stages of movement:

Yet, such an approach is incomplete, not systemic. If values and services move within economic space it would be more adequate to impose taxes along the entire route of the movement of media values and services.

Their cost is changeable depending upon the movement: the further we displace them, the more expensive they become.

Taxation in the process of production	Taxation in the process of distribution	Taxation in the process of exchange	Taxation in the process of consumption
Mass media values	Mass media values	Mass media values	Mass media values
Mass media services	Mass media services	Mass media services	Mass media services
The aggregate mass media product	The aggregate mass media product	The aggregate mass media product	The aggregate mass media product

B) The Mass Media Sphere and Services of the Judicial Power

The services of the judicial power are in a continuous interaction with that part of the activity which occurs beyond the frames outlined by the law. It is exposed to the impact of the «judicial instruments of influence».

The above can be displayed schematically as follows:

(Fig. 3)

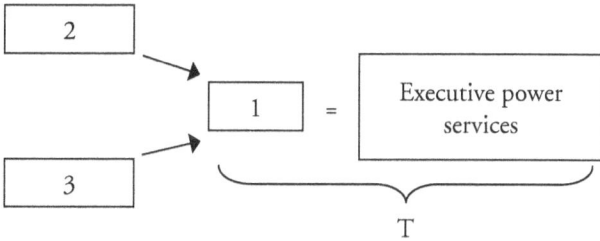

where

1—the mass media sphere as an economic system or, rather, that part of it where there are breaches of the law.

2—«Administrative—labor resources» of the judicial power;

3—Administrative instruments of the influence of the judicial power;

T—time spent on the creation of judicial power services.

I suggest that these breaches should be formalized and represented as a matrix—Δ—delta divergencies:

$$\begin{cases} -\Delta C_1 - \Delta V_1 - \Delta m_1 = -\Delta R_1 \\ -\Delta C_2 - \Delta V_2 - \Delta m_2 = -\Delta R_1 \end{cases}$$

Thus, the services of the judicial branch of power are created as a result of the interaction of the above factors:

-    specific implements of labor of the judicial branch of power;
-    specific subject of the labor of the judicial branch of power;
-    specific labor resources of the judicial branch of power.

The creation of the judicial services in the mass media sphere can be detailed as shown below:

(Fig. 4)

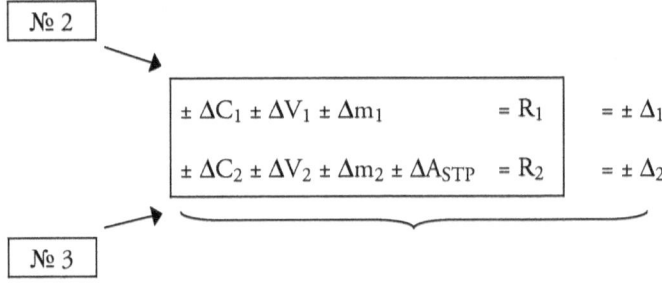

where

± Δ_1—lessening «-» or growing «+» of social evil (economic offences) within division I of the mass media sphere;

± Δ_2—lessening «-» or growing «+» of social evil (economic offences) within division II of the mass media sphere.

As suggested above from Fig. 4 reveals, on the one hand, the existence of media diverges from the law. They perform as a specific subject of labor for the judicial branch of power. But on the other hand the scheme shows the disposition of the administrative resource of the judiciary towards the illegal activity in the media.

Mass media values and services of illegal (criminal) origin move in a common economic space which can be represented as follows:

Production process	Distribution process	Exchange process	Consumption process
«-»Δ Mass media values	«-»Δ Mass media values	«-»Δ Mass media values	«-»Δ Mass media values
«-»Δ Mass media services	«-»Δ Mass media services	«-»Δ Mass media services	«-»Δ Mass media services
«-»Δ The aggregate mass media product	«-»Δ The aggregate mass media product	«-»Δ The aggregate mass media product	«-»Δ The aggregate mass media product

On every stage of the movement of mass media values and services (these possible Δ-divergencies) can be interpreted in the following way:

(Fig. 5)

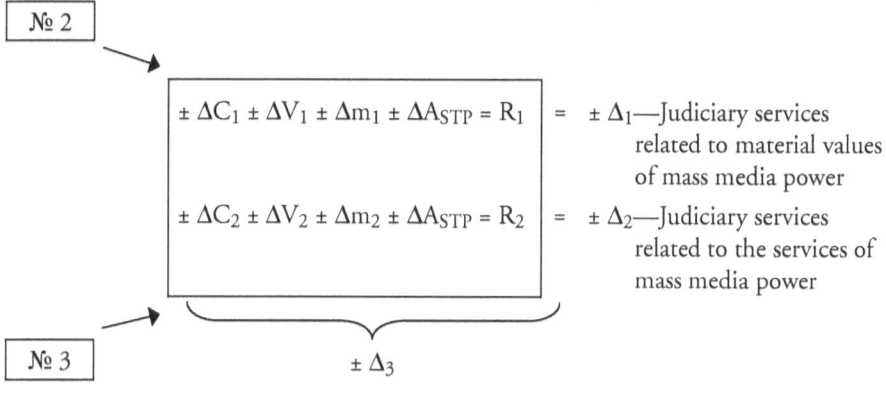

№ 2

$$\pm \Delta C_1 \pm \Delta V_1 \pm \Delta m_1 \pm \Delta A_{STP} = R_1$$

= $\pm \Delta_1$—Judiciary services related to material values of mass media power

$$\pm \Delta C_2 \pm \Delta V_2 \pm \Delta m_2 \pm \Delta A_{STP} = R_2$$

= $\pm \Delta_2$—Judiciary services related to the services of mass media power

№ 3

$\pm \Delta_3$

, where

$\pm \Delta_1$—judicial power services № 1;

$\pm \Delta_2$—judicial power services № 2;

$\pm \Delta_3$—complex judicial power services $\Delta_3 = (\pm \Delta_1 \pm \Delta_2)$

Provided that the three branches of power have a certain influence on the mass media sphere, we shall deduct (add up) these two quaternions.

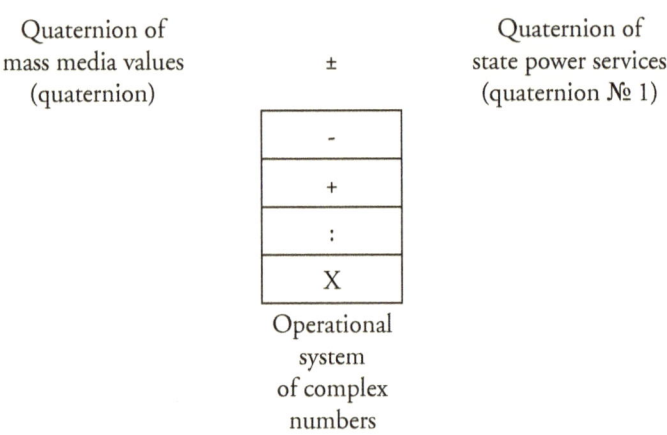

The next problem emerging here refers to the deduction (addition) of the «quaternion of state power services» and the «quaternion of mass media services».

For the deduction (or addition) of quaternion № 1 and № 2 it is necessary to use with complex numbers with the operations.

A)   Operational system of complex numbers

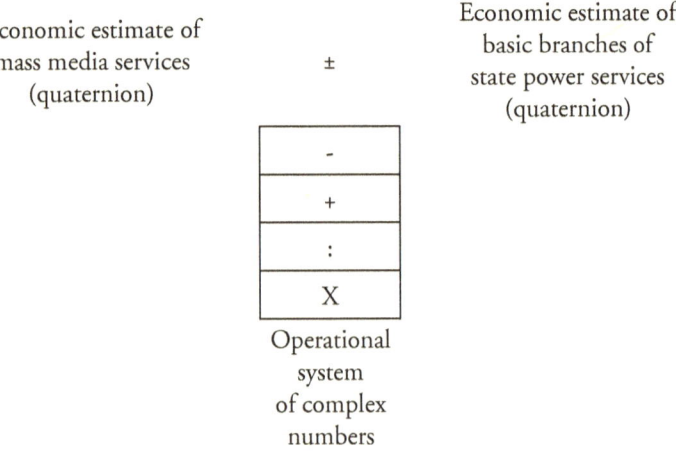

I suggest that the shifting of the power vector should be graphically shown as follows:

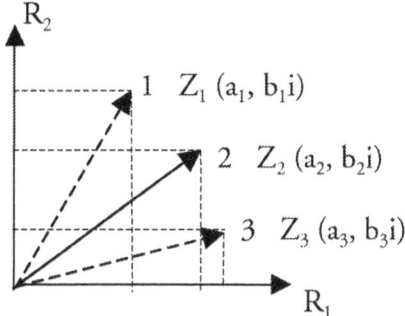

where,

- by placing the total vector of the three basic branches of state power «R_1» on axis «X»;
- by placing the total vector of the mass media «R_2» on axis «Y».

The position of vector Z_1 indicates that there has been a shift of state power towards the mass media.

The position of vector Z_2 testifies to the equality between the total mass media vector R_1 and the vector of the three main branches of state power R_2.

The position of vector Z_3 proves that the shift occurred towards the three branches of state power. We shall investigate this problem at a greater length.

I consider mass media sphere as an economic system consisting of two major, relatively autonomous subdivisions:

a) Subdivision I—production of mass media values;

b) Subdivision II—production of mass media services.

B) Radio services and services of the basic branches of state power

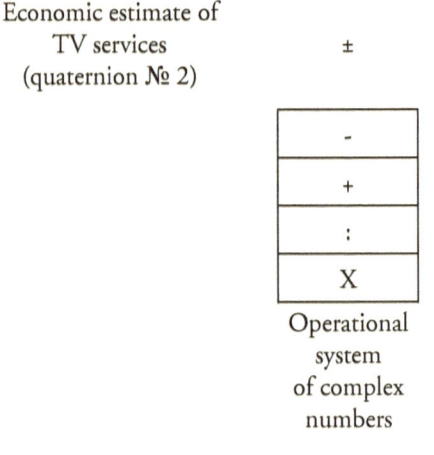

Economic estimate of
Radio services
(quaternion № 2)

±

Economic estimate of
the basic branches of
state power services
(quaternion № 1)

Operational
system
of complex
numbers

C) TV services and services of basic branches of state power

Economic estimate of
TV services
(quaternion № 2)

±

Economic estimate of
basic branches of
state power services
(quaternion № 1)

Operational
system
of complex
numbers

CHAPTER 7

The Movement of the Services of the Three Power Branches in Economic Space

We shall keep in mind that the services of the three main branches of power represent specific economic products created in the framework of socially organized state process. The movement of these products can be featured as follows:

Production process	Distribution process	Exchange process	Consumption process
Legislative power services	Legislative power services	Legislative power services	Legislative power services
Executive power services	Executive power services	Executive power services	Executive power services
Judicial power services	Judicial power services	Judicial power services	Judicial power services

Along with the above-mentioned the stream of services of the three main branches of power, mass media values and services are also moving in the economic space.

Production process	Distribution process	Exchange process	Consumption process
Mass media values	Mass media values	Mass media values	Mass media values
Mass media services	Mass media services	Mass media services	Mass media services
The aggregate mass media product	The aggregate mass media product	The aggregate mass media product	The aggregate mass media product

The movement of the mass media sphere is taking place along with the services of legislative, executive and judicial branches of power. The combined motion can be represented schematically as follows:

1. Production of services of the legislative power—A
2. Production of services of the executive power—B
3. Production of services of the judicial power—C

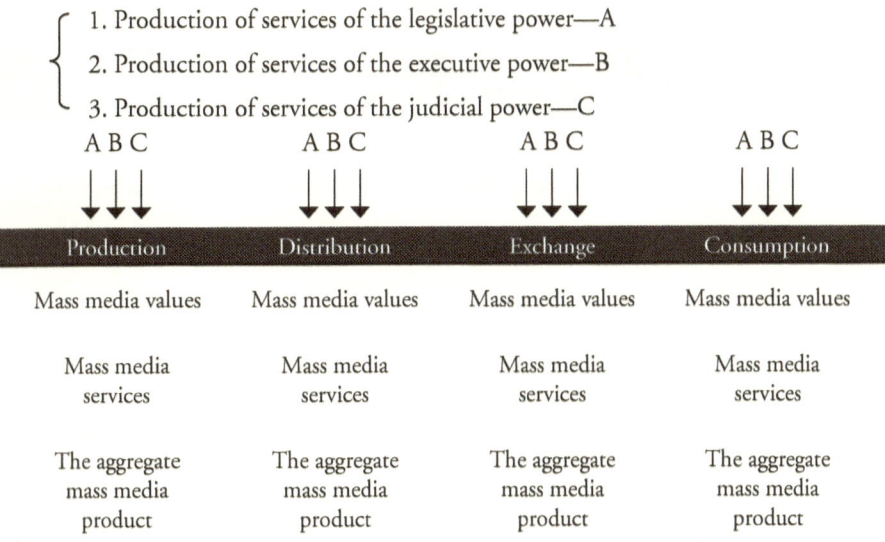

Production	Distribution	Exchange	Consumption
Mass media values	Mass media values	Mass media values	Mass media values
Mass media services	Mass media services	Mass media services	Mass media services
The aggregate mass media product	The aggregate mass media product	The aggregate mass media product	The aggregate mass media product

| Taxes | Taxes | Taxes | Taxes |

A—Laws—Legislative power services

1. Economic Estimates of Mass Media Values and Services Including State Power Services

The services of the three branches of state power directly affect the mass media sphere, the movement of its resources, the displacement of mass media values and services, exchange relations, and as well as the relations of the consumption of mass media values and services.

Mass media values and services move in economic space:

Process of production	Process of distribution	Process of exchange	Process of consumption
Values of the mass media	Values of the mass media	Values of the mass media	Values of the mass media
Services of the mass media	Services of the mass media	Services of the mass media	Services of the mass media
The aggregate mass media product	The aggregate mass media product	The aggregate mass media product	The aggregate mass media product

It is essential to take into economic account any influence of the power branches (whether they be positive or negative). Everything, without and exception, should be economically assessed.

In this part of the work we shall perform arithmetic operations with compound complex numbers, or rather, with economic estimates written with the use of complex numbers—quaternions.

Table 7.1

Economic estimate of creating mass media values $(C_1 + V_1 i + m_1 j)$	+	± «leg»—economic estimate of the influence of legislative power services on the process of creating mass media values
		± «exec»—economic estimate of the influence of executive power services on the process of creating mass media values
		± «jud»—economic estimate of the influence of judicial power services on the process of creating mass media values

Table 7.2

Economic estimate of creating mass media services $(C2 + V2i + m2j +$ ASSTP)	+	± «leg»—economic estimate of the influence of legislative power services on the process of creating mass media services
		± «exec»—economic estimate of the influence of executive power services on the process of creating mass media services
		± «jud»—economic estimate of the influence of judicial power services on the process of creating mass media services

Table 7.3

Economic estimate of creating the aggregate mass media product $(C_1 + V_1i + m_1j + + C_2 + V_2i + m_2j + A^S_{STP})$	+	± «leg»—economic estimate of the influence of legislative power services on the process of creating aggregate mass media product
		± «exec»—economic estimate of the influence of executive power services on the process of creating aggregate mass media product
		± «jud»—economic estimate of the influence of judicial power services on the process of creating aggregate mass media product

2. <u>Economic estimate of the distribution</u> of mass media values, services and the aggregate mass media product taking into account the influence of the services of the three branches of power.

Table 7.4

AA	Economic estimation of the distribution of mass media values	+	± «leg»—economic estimate of the influence of legislative power services on the process of distribution of mass media values
			± «exec»—economic estimate of the influence of executive power services on the process of distribution of mass media values
			± «jud»—economic estimate of the influence of judicial power services on the process of distribution of mass media values

BB	Economic estimation of the distribution of mass media services	+	± «leg»—economic estimate of the influence of legislative power services on the process of distribution of mass media services
			± «exec»—economic estimate of the influence of executive power services on the process of distribution of mass media services
			± «jud»—economic estimate of the influence of judicial power services on the process of distribution of mass media services
CC	Economic estimation of the distribution of the aggregate mass media product	+	± «leg»—economic estimate of the influence of legislative power services on the process of distribution of the aggregate mass media product
			± «exec»—economic estimate of the influence of executive power services on the process of the distribution of the aggregate mass media product
			± «jud»—economic estimate of the influence of judicial power services on the process of the distribution of the aggregate mass media product

3. <u>Economic estimate of the exchange</u> of mass media values, services and the aggregate mass media product taking into account the influence of the services of three branches of power.

Table 7.5

AA	Economic estimation of the exchange of mass media values	+	± «leg»—economic estimate of the influence of legislative power services on the process of the exchange of mass media values
			± «exec»—economic estimate of the influence of executive power services on the process of the exchange of mass media values
			± «jud»—economic estimate of the influence of judicial power services on the process of the exchange of mass media values

BB	Economic estimation of the exchange of mass media services	+	± «leg»—economic estimate of the influence of legislative power services on the process of the exchange of mass media services
			± «exec»—economic estimate of the influence of executive power services on the process of the exchange of mass media services
			± «jud»—economic estimate of the influence of judicial power services on the process of the exchange of mass media services
CC	Economic estimation of the exchange of the aggregate mass media product	+	± «leg»—economic estimate of the influence of legislative power services on the process of the exchange of the aggregate mass media product
			± «exec»—economic estimate of influence of executive power services on the process of the exchange of the aggregate mass media product
			± «jud»—economic estimate of influence of judicial power services on the process of the exchange of the aggregate mass media product

4. Economic estimate of consumption of mass media values, services and aggregate mass media product taking into account the influence of the services of the three branches of power.

Table 7.6

AA	Economic estimation of the consumption of mass media values	+	± «leg»—economic estimate of the influence of legislative power services on the process of the consumption of mass media values
			± «exec»—economic estimate of the influence of executive power services on the process of the consumption of mass media values
			± «jud»—economic estimate of the influence of judicial power services on the process of the consumption of mass media values

BB	Economic estimation of the consumption of mass media services	+	± «leg»—economic estimate of the influence of legislative power services on the process of the consumption of mass media services ± «exec»—economic estimate of the influence of executive power services on the process of the consumption of mass media services ± «jud»—economic estimate of the influence of judicial power services on the process of the consumption of mass media services
CC	Economic estimation of the consumption of the aggregate mass media product	+	± «leg»—economic estimate of the influence of legislative power services on the process of consumption of the aggregate mass media product ± «exec»—economic estimate of the influence of the executive power services on the process of consumption of the aggregate mass media product ± «jud»—economic estimate of the influence of judicial power services on the process of consumption of the aggregate mass media product

CHAPTER 8

The Taxation in the Mass Media Sphere

The use of complex numbers in calculation of mass media values (MMV) and mass media services (MMS) will prompt that the problem of taxation in the media sphere should be resolved with the aid of complex numbers.

In general, the outline of the taxation of media services can be shown in a three-dimensional space:

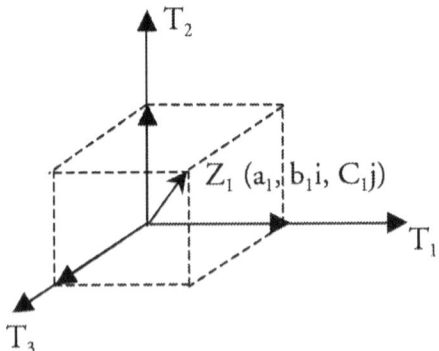

Where,

T_1—taxation of the depreciation funds—basic fund payments;

T_2—wage tax (direct labor in time);

T_3—assimilated resource tax (A_{STP}).

1. Taxation of Mass Media Values

1—System of taxes of division I

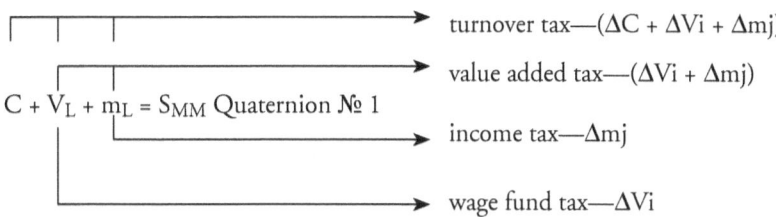

turnover tax—$(\Delta C + \Delta Vi + \Delta mj)$

value added tax—$(\Delta Vi + \Delta mj)$

$C + V_L + m_L = S_{MM}$ Quaternion № 1

income tax—Δmj

wage fund tax—ΔVi

2. Taxation of Mass Media Services

In general, a media service will be recorded as:

$$C + V + ResA_{STP} + m = SER_{MM} \text{ Quaternion № 2}$$

C—past labor expenses connected to the spare time of the population assimilated by the media services.

V—direct labor expenses connected to the creation of mass media services.

$ResA_{STP}$—people's spare time resources assimilated by the media services.

Ser_{MM}—the cost of the media services.

m—advertisement revenues.

In the mass media sphere the assimilated spare time of the population comes forward as an «attained resource».[25]

Provided the ASTP resources are included in the cost of media services the tax system will experience principal changes along with the widening basis of taxation.

T—as a tax on human resource the assimilated spare time (A_{STP}) should not evoke a negative reaction with the reader. Speaking of the existence of the wage tax or, in the other terms of an assimilated working time tax (V), why should not there be any form of tax imposed on the people's spare time, the time which is involved in the production process as a subject of labor?

---

[25]   2. Resource tax «spare time of the population assimilated by media services».

3. General Structure of the Taxation In The Sphere of Mass Media

Axiom 5. Proceeding from the assumption that the media sphere is comprised of two divisions that should logically exist two relatively independent groups of taxes.

1—System of taxes of division I

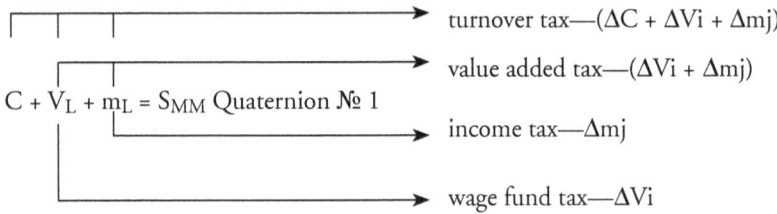

$C + V_L + m_L = S_{MM}$ Quaternion № 1

- turnover tax—$(\Delta C + \Delta Vi + \Delta mj)$
- value added tax—$(\Delta Vi + \Delta mj)$
- income tax—Δmj
- wage fund tax—ΔVi

2—System of taxes of division II

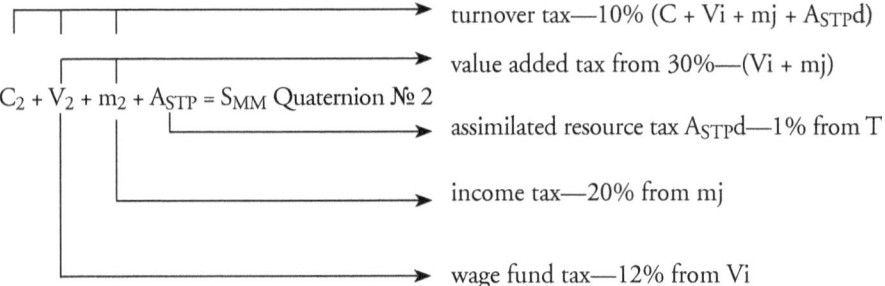

$C_2 + V_2 + m_2 + A_{STP} = S_{MM}$ Quaternion № 2

- turnover tax—10% $(C + Vi + mj + A_{STP}d)$
- value added tax from 30%—$(Vi + mj)$
- assimilated resource tax $A_{STP}d$—1% from T
- income tax—20% from mj
- wage fund tax—12% from Vi

3—Aggregate taxation system of mass media divisions I and II

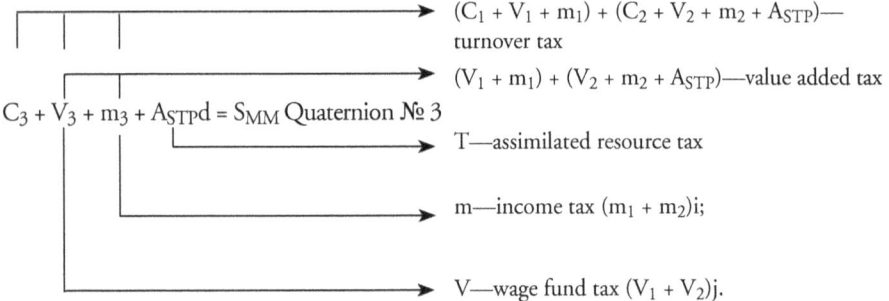

$C_3 + V_3 + m_3 + A_{STP}d = S_{MM}$ Quaternion № 3

- $(C_1 + V_1 + m_1) + (C_2 + V_2 + m_2 + A_{STP})$—turnover tax
- $(V_1 + m_1) + (V_2 + m_2 + A_{STP})$—value added tax
- T—assimilated resource tax
- m—income tax $(m_1 + m_2)i$;
- V—wage fund tax $(V_1 + V_2)j$.

Multiple media taxation may occur when resources become liable to manifold taxes.

1. V, m, $A_{ST}P$—first level taxes.
2. $(V + m)$—second level taxes (double taxation).
3. $(V + m + A_{STP})$—first level taxes (triple taxation).

Yet, such an approach is incomplete, not systemic. If values and services move within economic space it would be more adequate to impose taxes along the entire route of movement of the media values and services.[26]

Their cost is changeable depending upon the movement: the further we displace them the more expensive they become.

4. Problem with the Improvement of Mass Media Economic Mechanisms

As it has been pointed out above the economic theory of the mass media has not been elaborated yet. It remains at a deadlock. Indicators which have been used here, such as number of readers, radio listeners, TV viewers, have become obsolete: undersolved problems in the theory make the use of resources in the sphere of mass media ineffective.

The new approach in estimating the effectiveness of this sphere will make it possible to examine the economic mechanisms of the mass media from other angles.[27]

It is time to get over to precise economic calculations in the mass media sphere.

It can be implemented on the basis of political economic categories which have not been applied here before.

In this connection, I suggest to consider the mass media as an economic system with its specific relations.

The development of the mass media as an economic system implies first of all development of economic mechanisms of production, distribution, exchange and consumption.

---

[26] 4. TAXATION OF MASS MEDIA VALUES AND SERVICES ON EVERY STAGE OF THEIR MOVEMENT IN ECONOMIC SPACE

[27] I suggest that the aggregate mass media product should be evaluated within three-dimensional space:

Quaternion № 1 + Quaternion № 2 = Aggregate mass media product

Mechanism of production	Mechanism of distribution	Mechanism of exchange	Mechanism of consumption
Mass media values	Mass media values	Mass media values	Mass media values
Mass media services	Mass media services	Mass media services	Mass media services
The mass media aggregate product	The mass media aggregate product	The mass media aggregate product	The mass media aggregate product

We shall start investigating the problems of the mass media sphere by considering the mechanisms of the movement of the «means of labor» and «tools of labor», «labor resources», «subject of labor», all these within economic relations of:

- production;
- distribution;
- exchange;
- consumption.

5. Economic Relations within Mass Media

A_1

Stream of resources		
Means of labor		
Tools of labor	Production	Mass media values
Labor resources		
Subject of labor		

A_2

Stream of resources		
Means of labor		
Tools of labor	Distribution	Mass media values
Labor resources		
Subject of labor		

A_3

Stream of resources		
Means of labor		
Tools of labor	Exchange	Mass media values
Labor resources		
Subject of labor		

A_4

Stream of resources		
Means of labor		
Tools of labor	Consumption	Mass media values
Labor resources		
Subject of labor		

B_1

Stream of resources		
Means of labor		
Tools of labor	Production	Mass media services
Labor resources		
Subject of labor		

B$_2$

Stream of resources		
Means of labor		
Tools of labor	Distribution	Mass media services
Labor resources		
Subject of labor		

B$_3$

Stream of resources		
Means of labor		
Tools of labor	Exchange	Mass media services
Labor resources		
Subject of labor		

B$_4$

Stream of resources		
Means of labor		
Tools of labor	Consumption	Mass media services
Labor resources		
Subject of labor		

C$_1$

Stream of resources		
Means of labor		
Tools of labor	Production	The aggregate mass media product
Labor resources		
Subject of labor		

C_2

Stream of resources		
Means of labor		
Tools of labor	Distribution	The aggregate mass media product
Labor resources		
Subject of labor		

C_3

Stream of resources		
Means of labor		
Tools of labor	Exchange	The aggregate mass media product
Labor resources		
Subject of labor		

C_4

Stream of resources		
Means of labor		
Tools of labor	Consumption	Aggregate mass media product
Labor resources		
Subject of labor		

Economic relations and process within the mass media sphere are not entirely flawless. Imperfection of certain relations entail definite disproportions which can be judged by the following.

Given that one of the elements is absent the system will not represent an integral formation. This becomes apparent if the subject of labor, in the capacity of a radio listener, a TV viewer, is absent. Such a case will imply that media services are not consumed for the absence of a consumer.

That is why it has become necessary to improve the economic mechanism of the mass media.

Improvement of production mechanism	Improvement of distribution mechanism	Improvement of consumption mechanism	Improvement of exchange mechanism
Improvement of the production mechanism of mass media values	Improvement of the distribution mechanism of mass media values	Improvement of the consumption mechanism of mass media values	Improvement of the exchange mechanism of mass media values
Improvement of the production mechanism of mass media services	Improvement of the distribution mechanism of mass media services	Improvement of the consumption mechanism of mass media services	Improvement of the exchange mechanism of mass media services
Improvement of the production mechanism of the mass media aggregate product	Improvement of the distribution mechanism of the mass media aggregate product	Improvement of the consumption mechanism of the mass media aggregate product	Improvement of the exchange mechanism of the mass media aggregate product

CHAPTER 9

The Influence of the Mass Media on the Basic Branches of State Power

The mass media sphere is expanding and is replacing the position the «traditional» branches of state power. As professor P. Reeves says: «For the last few years there has been a shift of the power towards the mass media».

Where does the state power move?

What happens within it?

To answer this question we shall have specific economic estimates, criteria, indicators for each of the power branches.

Professor Reeves insists that the state power has shifted toward the mass media although he is not definite about the exact area of the shift whether it is in TV, radio or press industry. He does not specify the real implication of the state power vector. We might equally well state the contrary: we can. maintain that the shift of the state power has happened in the direction just opposite of the mass media.[28]

That is why we shall make it clear as to:

- what is the quality of the change of the power vector which has happened under the influence of newspaper industry?

---

[28] The mass media sphere can either accelerate or slow down the social and economic processes in the society. It determines the shifts and turnings in the dynamics of the movement of a state.

What is happening in the state power sphere? What economic estimates, criteria and indicators are used here? We have to investigate everything that concerns the state authority.

- what is the quality of the change of the power vector which has taken place under the influence of radio?
- what is the quality of the change of the power vector which has resulted under the influence of Television?

The mass media is capable of exerting particular pressure on the main branches of state power (A, B, C). This impact can either widen or narrow specific services of legislative, executive and judicial character. The mass media can severely «bite» the main branches of power. The latter, however, is capable of healing the wounds very quickly.

This problem has been laid into the plot of B. Levinson's film with a suggestive title «When the tail wags the dog» (Wag the Dog).

The film is a narrative of a paradoxical situation when some of the dog's limbs change their functional meaning—the tail is wagging the dog (the basic power branches become secondary and vice versa).

Yet everything becomes properly disposed as soon as you have watched the film. You understand that ordinary citizens perform the role of the dog, whereas the tail or, rather, mass media, is manipulating the public.

It also becomes evident that the legislative, executive and judicial powers get so compressed by the media that they become almost invisible.

The impact of the vector shift of the media on the movements of the services of the main branches of power in the economic space can be interpreted as follows:

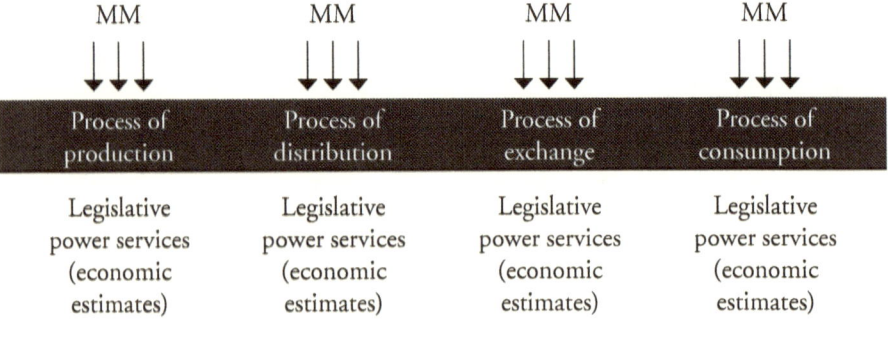

Process of production	Process of distribution	Process of exchange	Process of consumption
Executive power services (economic estimates)	Executive power services (economic estimates)	Executive power services (economic estimates)	Executive power services (economic estimates)
Judicial power services (economic estimates)	Judicial power services (economic estimates)	Judicial power services (economic estimates)	Judicial power services (economic estimates)

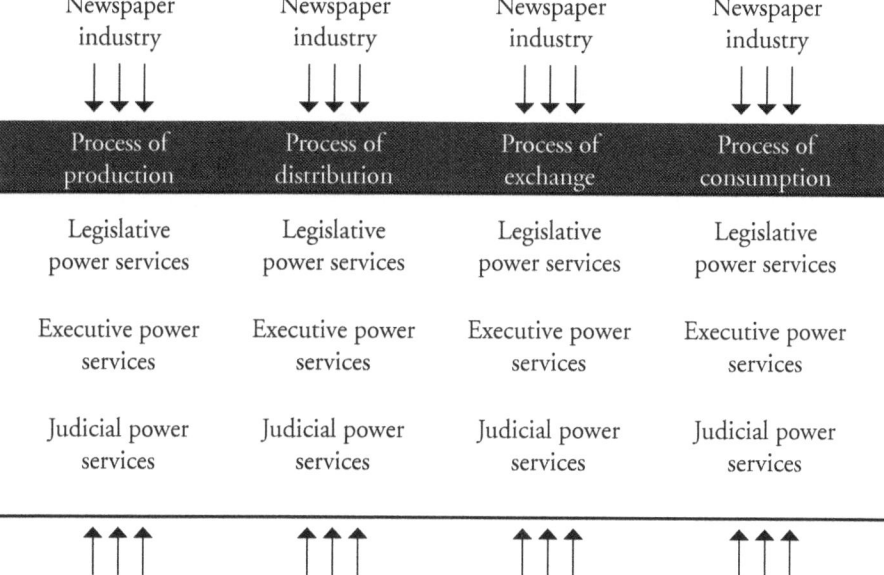

The magnitude of the shifting of the power vector should be examined in the context of:

- impact of newspaper industry on the vector of legislative power;
- impact of newspaper industry on the vector of executive power;
- impact of newspaper industry on the vector of judicial power;

Newspaper industry	Newspaper industry	Newspaper industry	Newspaper industry

Process of production	Process of distribution	Process of exchange	Process of consumption
Legislative power services	Legislative power services	Legislative power services	Legislative power services
Executive power services	Executive power services	Executive power services	Executive power services
Judicial power services	Judicial power services	Judicial power services	Judicial power services

1. Economic estimate of first type

Economic estimate of creating legislative power services		± A—economic estimate of the influence of the newspaper industry on the legislative branch of power;
Economic estimate of creating executive power services	+	± B—economic estimate of the influence of the newspaper industry on the executive branch of power;
Economic estimate of creating judicial power services		± C—economic estimate of the influence of the newspaper industry on the judicial branch of power.

2. Economic estimate of second type

Economic estimate of the distribution of legislative power services		± A—economic estimate of the influence of the newspaper industry on the legislative branch of power;
Economic estimate of the distribution of executive power services	+	± B—economic estimate of the influence of the newspaper industry on the executive branch of power;
Economic estimate of the distribution of judicial power services		± C—economic estimate of the influence of the newspaper industry on the judicial branch of power.

3. Economic estimate of third type

Economic estimate of the exchange of legislative power services		± A—economic estimate of the influence of the newspaper industry on the legislative branch of power;
Economic estimate of the exchange of executive power services	+	± B—economic estimate of the influence of the newspaper industry on the executive branch of power;
Economic estimate of the exchange of judicial power services		± C—economic estimate of the influence of the newspaper industry on the judicial branch of power.

4.   Economic estimate of fourth type

Economic estimate of the consumption of legislative power services		± A—economic estimate of the influence of the newspaper industry on the legislative branch of power;
Economic estimate of the consumption of executive power services	+	± B—economic estimate of the influence of the newspaper industry on the executive branch of power;
Economic estimate of the consumption of judicial power services		± C—economic estimate of the influence of the newspaper industry on the judicial branch of power.

The magnitude of the shifting of the power vector should be examined in the context of:

- the impact of the radio of the vector on legislative power;
- the impact of the radio of the vector on executive power;
- the impact of the radio of the vector on judicial power;

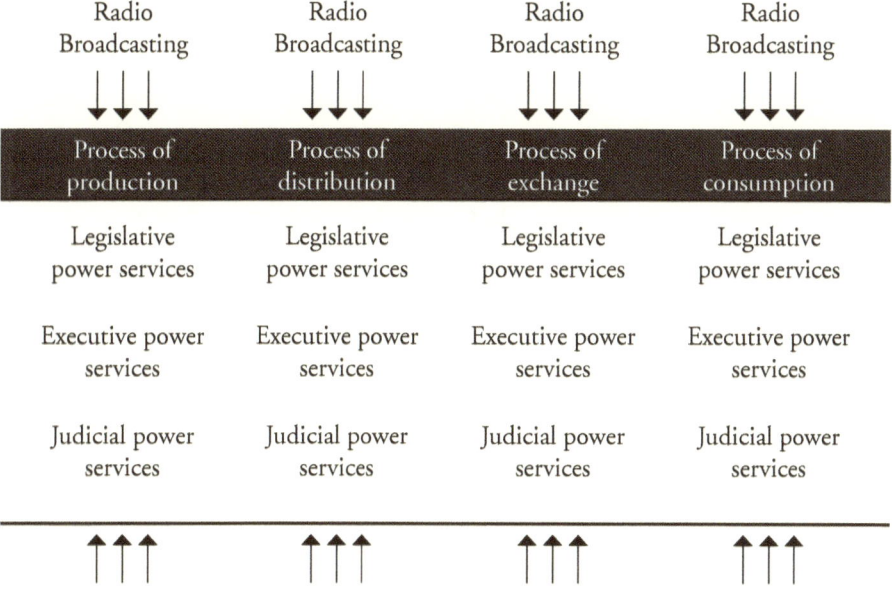

Economic estimate of creating legislative power services		± AA—economic estimate of the influence of radio broadcasting services on the legislative of power;
Economic estimate of creating executive power services	+	± BB—economic estimate of the influence of radio broadcasting services on the executive of power;
Economic estimate of creating judicial power services		± CC—economic estimate of the influence of radio broadcasting services on the judicial of power.

Economic estimate of the distribution of legislative power services		± AA—economic estimate of the influence of radio broadcasting services on the legislative of power;
Economic estimate of the distribution of executive power services	+	± BB—economic estimate of the influence of radio broadcasting services on the executive of power;
Economic estimate of the distribution of judicial power services		± CC—economic estimate of the influence of radio broadcasting services on the judicial of power.

Economic estimate of the exchange of legislative power services		± AA—economic estimate of the influence of radio broadcasting services on the legislative of power;
Economic estimate of the exchange of executive power services	+	± BB—economic estimate of the influence of radio broadcasting services on the executive of power;
Economic estimate of the exchange of judicial power services		± CC—economic estimate of the influence of radio broadcasting services on the judicial of power.

Economic estimate of the consumption of legislative power services		± AA—economic estimate of the influence of radio broadcasting services on the legislative of power;
Economic estimate of the consumption of executive power services	+	± BB—economic estimate of the influence of radio broadcasting services on the executive of power;
Economic estimate of the consumption of judicial power services		± CC—economic estimate of the influence of radio broadcasting services on the judicial of power.

The magnitude of the shifting of the power vector should be examined in the context of:

- the impact of TV on the vector of legislative power;
- the impact of TV on the vector of executive power;
- the impact of TV on the vector of judicial power.

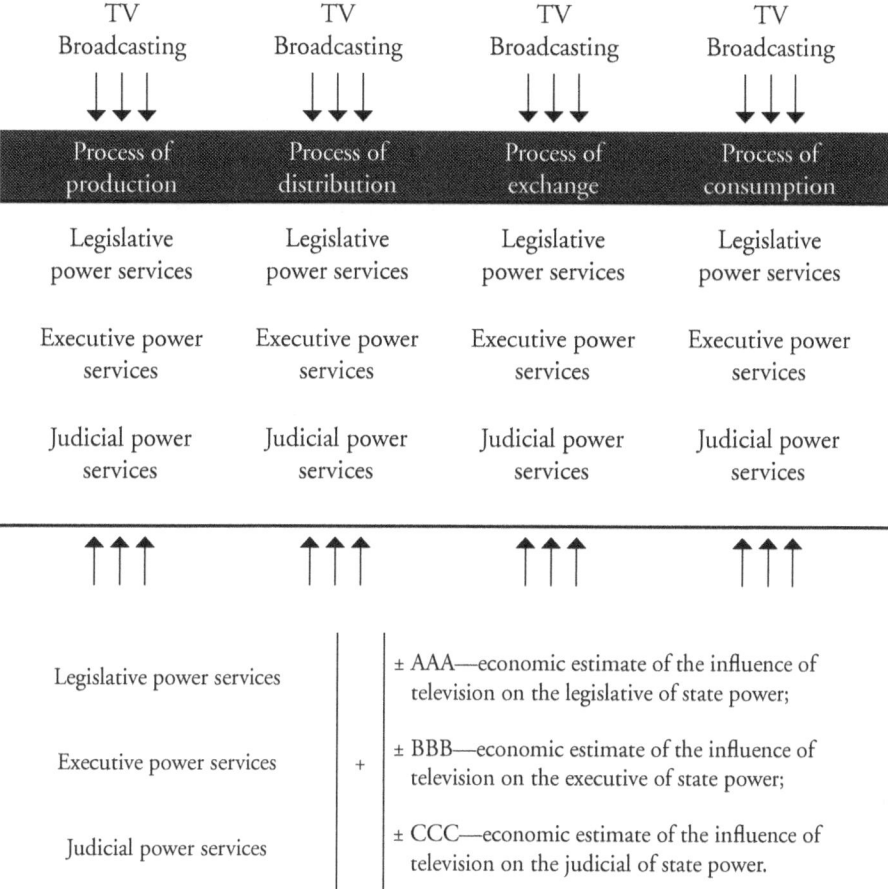

Legislative power services		± AAA—economic estimate of the influence of television on the legislative of state power;
Executive power services	+	± BBB—economic estimate of the influence of television on the executive of state power;
Judicial power services		± CCC—economic estimate of the influence of television on the judicial of state power.
Legislative power services		± AAA—economic estimate of the influence of television on the legislative of state power;
Executive power services	+	± BBB—economic estimate of the influence of television on the executive of state power;
Judicial power services		± CCC—economic estimate of the influence of television on the judicial of state power.
Legislative power services		± AAA—economic estimate of the influence of television on the legislative of state power;
Executive power services	+	± BBB—economic estimate of the influence of television on the executive of state power;
Judicial power services		± CCC—economic estimate of the influence of television on the judicial of state power.

± AAAA—economic estimate of the influence of the three branches of power on newspapers;

± BBBB—economic estimate of the influence of the three branches of power on the radio;

± CCCC—economic estimate of the influence of the three branches of power on television.

CHAPTER 10

The Peculiarities of the Stock Exchange Index for the Mass Media Sphere

1. Calculation of Expenses Connected with Consumption of the Aggregate Mass Media Product

Mass media needs are being met along two interopposed planes:

- part of the mass media needs have production character;
- part of the mass media needs are of non-production character.

In general the structure of production needs of mass media values and services are as follows:

a) production needs in mass media values;

b) production needs in mass media services;

c) production needs in the aggregate mass media product.

Non-production character of meeting mass media needs has the following structure:

a) non-production needs in mass media values;

b) non-production needs in mass media services;

c) non-production needs in the aggregate mass media product.

The above mentioned can be interpreted by the following logical table:

Production consumption	Non-production consumption	Aggregate consumption
Mass media values	Mass media values	Mass media values
Mass media services	Mass media services	Mass media services
The aggregate mass media product	The aggregate mass media product	The aggregate mass media product

All the volume of an aggregate mass media product is divided into the values and services of production consumption and into the values and services of non-production consumption.

Mass media production created in Division I (material form)

$$C_1 + V_1 i + m_1 j = Z_1$$

, where

C_1—expenses of past labor connected to the newly created mass media values;

V_1—wages of the employees connected to the creation of mass media values;

m_1—profit obtained out of the creation of mass media values.

Mass media production created in Division II (service form)

$$C_2 + V_2 i + m_2 j + A_{STP} k = Z_2$$

$$C_2 + V_2 i + m_2 j + A_{STP} k = \text{mass media services}$$

, where

C_2—expenses of past labor connected to the creation of mass media services;

$V_2 i$—wages of employees connected to the creation of mass media service;

$m_2 j$—income from the activity;

$A_{STP} k$—assimilated resource of the spare time of population mass media services.

Aggregate mass media production created in Divisions I & II

$$(C_1 + C_2) + (V_1 + V_2)i + (m_1 + m_2)j + A_{STP}k = Z_3$$

The above mentioned can be systematically presented like this:

1) The mass media values created in Division I are distributed in four directions:

    1. The mass media values of a production purpose for Division I;
    2. The mass media values of a production purpose for Division II;
    3. The mass media values of non-production purpose for Division I;
    4. The mass media values of non-production purpose for Division II;

    Non-production consumption mass media values

1) $C_1 + \Delta V_1^{P}i + \Delta V_1^{NP}i + \Delta m_1^{P}j + \Delta m_1^{NP}j = R_1$

    Production consumption

where

$\Delta V_1^{P}i$—partial wages of production character

$\Delta V_1^{NP}i$—partial wages of non-production character

$\Delta m_1^{P}j$—partial profit obtained activities of production character

$\Delta m_1^{NP}j$—partial profit obtained activities of non-production character

1. Mass media values

Branches	Volume of mass media values (production use)				Volume of mass media values (non-production use)				Aggregate volume of mass media values				Estimations	Criteria	Indicators
	№ 1	№ 2	№ 3	№ 4	№ 5	№ 6	№ 7	№ 8	№ 9	№ 10	№ 11	№ 12			
	▓												Estimations	Criteria	Indicators
		▓											Estimations	Criteria	Indicators
I branch			▓										Estimations	Criteria	Indicators
Production needs in values of the mass media sphere (estimation)				▓									Estimations	Criteria	Indicators
					▓								Estimations	Criteria	Indicators
						▓							Estimations	Criteria	Indicators
II branch							▓						Estimations	Criteria	Indicators
Non-production needs in values of the mass media sphere (estimation)								▓					Estimations	Criteria	Indicators
									▓				Estimations	Criteria	Indicators
										▓			Estimations	Criteria	Indicators
III branch											▓		Estimations	Criteria	Indicators
Complex needs in values of the mass media sphere (estimation)												▓	Estimations	Criteria	Indicators
													Estimations	Criteria	Indicators

2. Mass media services

2) The mass media services created in Division II are distributed in four directions:

1. The mass media services of a production purpose for Division I;
2. The mass media services of a production purpose for Division II;
3. The mass media services of a non-production purpose for Division I;
4. The mass media services of a non-production purpose for Division II.

Non-production consumption mass media services

2) $C_2 + \Delta V_2{}^{P}i + \Delta V_2{}^{NP}i + \Delta m_2{}^{P}j + \Delta m_2{}^{NP}j + A_{STP}k = R_2$

Production consumption

where

$\Delta V_1{}^{P}i$—partial wages of production character

$\Delta V_1{}^{NP}i$—partial wages of non-production character

$\Delta m_1{}^{P}j$—partial profit obtained activities of production character

$\Delta m_1{}^{NP}j$—partial profit obtained activities of non-production character

1. Mass media services

Branches	Volume of mass media services (production use)				Volume of mass media services (non-production use)				Aggregate volume of mass media services						
	№ 1	№ 2	№ 3	№ 4	№ 5	№ 6	№ 7	№ 8	№ 9	№ 10	№ 11	№ 12	Estimations	Criteria	Indicators
													Estimations	Criteria	Indicators
													Estimations	Criteria	Indicators
													Estimations	Criteria	Indicators
													Estimations	Criteria	Indicators
I branch	Production needs in services of the mass media sphere (estimation)												Estimations	Criteria	Indicators
													Estimations	Criteria	Indicators
													Estimations	Criteria	Indicators
													Estimations	Criteria	Indicators
II branch					Non-production needs in services of the mass media sphere (estimation)								Estimations	Criteria	Indicators
													Estimations	Criteria	Indicators
													Estimations	Criteria	Indicators
													Estimations	Criteria	Indicators
III branch									Complex needs in services of the mass media sphere (estimation)				Estimations	Criteria	Indicators
													Estimations	Criteria	Indicators

The resource streams going out of the mass media sphere may be written as logical schemes:

Thesis   Mass media values of a production purpose for Division I

Antithesis   Mass media values of a production purpose for Division II

Synthesis   Aggregate volume of the mass media values, which are consumed within mass media sphere Divisions I & II for a production purpose

Thesis   Mass media values of a non-production purpose for Division I

Antithesis   Mass media values of a non-production purpose for Division II

Synthesis   Aggregate mass media values for Divisions I & II for a non-production purpose

Thesis   Mass media services of a production purpose for Division I

Antithesis   Mass media services of a production purpose for Division II

Synthesis   Aggregate volume of the mass media services, which are consumed within the mass media sphere Divisions I & II for a production purpose

Thesis   Mass media services of a non-production purpose for Division I

Antithesis   Mass media services of a non-production purpose for Division II

Synthesis   Aggregate volume of the mass media services for Divisions I & II for a non-production purpose

SYSTEM OF INDICATORS OF «LONG-TERM PROVISION» OF MASS MEDIA SERVICES (FUNCTIONAL INDICATION)

Thesis   Dialectical structure of a division of the aggregate of mass media services as per functional indication.

Thesis   An increment (Δ) of the volume of the mass media services for a production purpose.

Antithesis   An increment (Δ) of the volume of the mass media services for a non-production purpose.

Synthesis   An increment (Δ) of the volume of the aggregate mass media services.

Antithesis   Dialectical structure of needs for mass media services

Thesis   An increment (Δ) of the production needs in mass media services.

Antithesis   An increment (Δ) of the non-production needs in mass media services.

Synthesis   An increment (Δ) of the aggregate needs of a society in mass media services.

Synthesis   Dialectical system of the criteria of the «provision» with mass media services.

Thesis	$\dfrac{\text{An increment } (\Delta) \text{ of the volume of mass media services for a production purpose}}{\text{An increment } (\Delta) \text{ of the production needs}} =$	an indicator of the «long-term provision» of production purpose
Antithesis	$\dfrac{\text{An increment } (\Delta) \text{ of volume of the mass media services for a non-production purpose}}{\text{An increment } (\Delta) \text{ of non-production needs}} =$	an indicator of the «long-term provision» of a non-production purpose
Synthesis	$\dfrac{\text{An increment } (\Delta) \text{ of an aggregate volume of mass media services}}{\text{An increment } (\Delta) \text{ of aggregate needs}} =$	a complex indicator of the «long-term mass media provision»

Indicators of the Long-Term Provision of Mass Media Values and Services

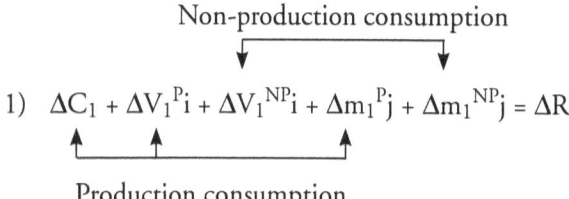

1) $\Delta C_1 + \Delta V_1^{P}i + \Delta V_1^{NP}i + \Delta m_1^{P}j + \Delta m_1^{NP}j = \Delta R_1$

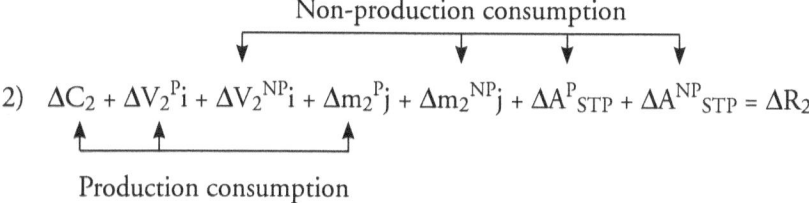

2) $\Delta C_2 + \Delta V_2^{P}i + \Delta V_2^{NP}i + \Delta m_2^{P}j + \Delta m_2^{NP}j + \Delta A^{P}_{STP} + \Delta A^{NP}_{STP} = \Delta R_2$

Production consumption

A System of the Criteria of the Effective Utilization of the Resources in the Mass Media Sphere (With Complex Numbers—Quaternions)

a) A system of effective criteria formed up a «results-expenses» principle:

1. «Thesis» criterion = $\dfrac{\text{results}}{\text{past labor expenses}}$

2. «Antithesis» criterion = $\dfrac{\text{results}}{\text{direct labor expenses}}$

3. «Synthesis» criterion = $\dfrac{\text{results}}{\text{aggregate labor expenses}}$

A system of criteria of the effective utilization of resources in the mass media production formed on the basis of «Gross Domestic Product» created in mass media sphere (GDP-MM-SP):

1. «Thesis» criterion = $\dfrac{(C + Vi + mj)\text{—quaternion}}{\text{Expenses of the past labor}\ (C)\text{—real number}}$

2. «Antithesis» criterion =

$$\frac{(C + Vi + mj)\text{—quaternion}}{\text{Expenses of the direct labor} \atop (Vi)\text{—imaginary number}}$$

3. «Synthesis» criterion =

$$\frac{(C + Vi + mj)\text{—quaternion}}{\text{Expenses of the aggregate} \atop \text{labor } (C + Vi)\text{—complex number}}$$

b) A system of criteria of the effective utilization of resources in the mass media production formed on the basis of «Net Domestic Product» created in mass media production (NDP-MM-SP)(Vi + mj) indicator:

1. «Thesis» criterion =

$$\frac{(Vi + mj)\text{—complex number}}{\text{Expenses of the past labor} \atop (C)\text{—real numbers}}$$

2. «Antithesis» criterion =

$$\frac{(Vi + mj)\text{—complex number}}{\text{Expenses of the direct labor} \atop (Vi)\text{—imaginary number}}$$

3. «Synthesis» criterion =

$$\frac{(Vi + mj)\text{—complex number}}{\text{Expenses of the aggregate} \atop \text{labor } (C + Vi)\text{—complex number}}$$

c) A system of criteria of the effective utilization of resources in the mass media production formed on the basis of «Net Income» created in mass media production (NI-MM) indicator:

1. «Thesis» criterion =

$$\frac{(mj)\text{—imaginary number}}{\text{Expenses of the past labor} \atop (C)\text{—real numbers}}$$

2. «Antithesis» criterion =

$$\frac{(mj)\text{—imaginary number}}{\text{Expenses of the direct labor} \atop (Vi)\text{—imaginary numbers}}$$

3. «Synthesis» criterion =

$$\frac{(mj)\text{—imaginary number}}{\text{Expenses of the aggregate} \atop \text{labor } (C + Vi)\text{—complex number}}$$

d) A system of the criteria of the effective utilization of the resources in the mass media production formed on the basis of the «assimilated resource of population spare time» ($AR_{STP}K$) indicator:

1. «Thesis» criterion = $\dfrac{AR_{STP}K\text{—imaginary number}}{\text{Expenses of the past labor}\atop{(C)\text{—real numbers}}}$

2. «Antithesis» criterion = $\dfrac{AR_{STP}K\text{—imaginary number}}{\text{Expenses of the direct labor}\atop{(Vi)\text{—imaginary numbers}}}$

3. «Synthesis» criterion = $\dfrac{AR_{STP}K\text{—imaginary number}}{\text{Expenses of the aggregate}\atop{\text{labor }(C + Vi)\text{—complex number}}}$

Scheme № 1

General Logical Scheme of the Criterion of the Effective Utilisation of Past Labor (Formed on the Basis of Category «Gross Domestic Product»)

A) Logical Scheme of the Criterion Of Effective Utilisation of Past Labor in Division I

Thesis GDP created in mass media sphere Division I ($C_1 + V_1i + m_1j$).

Antithesis Past labor expenses in Division I (C_1)

Synthesis $\dfrac{C_1 + V_1i + m_1j}{C1}$

B) Logical Scheme of the Criterion of Effective Utilisation of Past Labor in Division II

Thesis GDP created in mass media sphere Division II
($C_2 + V_2i + A^{MM}{}_{STP}k + m_2j$)

Antithesis Past labor expenses in Division II (C_2)

Synthesis $\dfrac{C_2 + V_2i + A^{MM}{}_{STP}k + m_2j}{C_2}$

C) **Logical Scheme of the Aggregate Criterion of Effective Utilisation of Past Labor in Divisions I, II**

Thesis	GDP created in mass media production Divisions I & II. $(C_1 + V_1i + m_1j) + (C_2 + V_2i + A^{MM}_{STP}k + m_2j)$
Antithesis	Past labor expenses in Divisions I & II. $(C_1 + C_2)$
Synthesis	$$\frac{(C_1 + V_1i + m_1j) + (C_2 + V_2i + A^{MM}_{STP}k + m_2j)}{C_1 + C_2}$$

Scheme № 2

Aggregate Scheme of the Criterion of the Effective Utilisation of Direct Labor as a Whole (Formed on the Basis of Category «Net Domestic Product»)

A) **Logical Scheme of the Criterion of Effective Utilisation of Direct Labor in Division I**

Thesis	NDP created in mass media sphere Division I $(V_1i + m_1j)$
Antithesis	Direct labor expenses in Division I (V_1i)
Synthesis	$$\frac{V_1i + m_1j}{V_1i}$$

B) **Logical Scheme of the Criterion of Effective Utilisation of Direct Labor in Division II**

Thesis	NDP created in mass media sphere Division II $(V_2i + A^{MM}_{STP}k + m_2j)$
Antithesis	Direct labor expenses in Division II (V_2i).
Synthesis	$$\frac{V_2i + A^{MM}_{STP}k + m_2j}{V_2i}$$

C) **Logical Scheme of the Criterion of Effective Utilisation of Direct Labor in Divisions I &II**

Thesis   NDP created in mass media production Divisions I & II
$$(V_1i + m_1j + V_2i + m_2j + A^{MM}_{STP}k)$$

Antithesis   Expenses of the direct labor in the mass media sphere Divisions I & II $(V_1i + V_2i)$

Synthesis $$\frac{V_1i + m_1j + V_2i + m_2j + A^{MM}_{STP}k}{V_1i + V_2i}$$

Scheme № 3

Aggregate Scheme of the Criterion of the Effective Utilisation of Direct Labor as a Whole (Formed on the Basis of Category «Net Income»)

A) **Logical Scheme of the Criterion of the Effective Utilisation of Direct Labor in Division I**

Thesis   NI created in mass media sphere Division I. (m_1j)

Antithesis   Direct labor expenses in Division I (V_1i).

Synthesis $$\frac{m_1j}{V_1i}$$

B) **Logical Scheme of the Criterion of the Effective Utilisation of Direct Labor in Division II**

Thesis   NI created in mass media sphere Division II. $(m_2j + A^{MM}_{STP}k)$

Antithesis   Direct labor expenses in Division II (V_2i).

Synthesis $$\frac{m_2j + A^{MM}_{STP}k}{V_2i}$$

C) Logical Scheme of the Criterion of the Effective Utilisation of Direct Labor in Divisions I, II & III

Thesis	NI created in mass media sphere Divisions I, II & III $(m_1j + A^{MM}_{STP}k + m_2j)$
Antithesis	Direct labor expenses in Divisions I & II $(V_1i + V_2i)$
Synthesis	$\dfrac{m_1j + A^{MM}_{STP}k + m_2j}{V_1i + V_2i}$

<u>Scheme № 4</u>

Aggregate Scheme of the Formation of the Criterion of the Effective Utilisation of Direct Labor As A Whole (Formed on the Basis of Category «Assimilated Resource of the Spare Time of Population»)

A) Logical Scheme of the Criterion of the Effective Utilisation of Direct Laborin Division I

Thesis	Assimilated resource of STP created in mass media sphere Division I (m_1j)
Antithesis	Direct labor expenses in Division I (V_1i)
Synthesis	$\dfrac{m_1j}{V_1i}$ $m_1j = 0$

B) Logical Scheme of the Criterion of the Effective Utilisation of Direct Labor in Division II

Thesis	Assimilated resource of STP within branches of Division II $(A^{MM}_{STP}k)$
Antithesis	Direct labor expenses in Division II (V_2i)
Synthesis	$\dfrac{A^{MM}_{STP}k}{V_2i}$

C) Logical Scheme of the Criterion of the Effective Utilisation of Direct Labor in Divisions I & II

Thesis   Assimilated resource of STP within branches of Divisions II
($A^{MM}_{STP}k$)

Antithesis   Direct labor expenses in Divisions I & II ($V_1i + V_2i$)

Synthesis $$\frac{A^{MM}_{STP}k}{V_1i + V_2i + V_3i}$$

Scheme № 5

Dialectical Structure
of Labor Expenses in the Mass Media Sphere

Thesis   Past labor expenses in a social process of the mass media product.

Antithesis   Direct labor expenses in a social process of the mass media product.

Synthesis   Aggregate labor expenses in a social process of mass media production, which synthesises social expenses of past and direct labor simultaneously.

Indicators of Mass Media Production Divisions I & II

MM-SP Division I

$C_1 + V_1i + m_1j$ —GDP_1 created in mass media sphere of Division I

$V_1i + m_1j$ —NDP_1 created in mass media sphere of Division I

m_1j —NI_1 created in mass media sphere of Division I

MM-SP Division II

$$C_2 + V_2i + A^{MM}_{STP}k + m_2j \quad —GDP_2 \text{ created in mass media sphere of Division II}$$

$$V_2i + A^{MM}_{STP}k + m_2j \quad —NDP_2 \text{ created in mass media sphere of Division II}$$

$$A^{MM}_{STP}k + m_2j \quad —NI_2 \text{ created in mass media sphere of Division II}$$

$$A^{MM}_{STP}k \quad —\text{assimilated resource STP within branches of Division II}$$

Scheme № 6

Dialectical Scheme of the Criteria of the Aggregate Effective Utilisation of Direct Labor in the Mass Media Sphere as a Whole (Formed on the Basis of Category «Gross Domestic Product»)

Thesis $\dfrac{GDP_1 + GDP_2}{C_1 + C_2}$ —capital return

Antithesis $\dfrac{GDP_1 + GDP_2}{V_1i + V_2i}$ —productivity of a direct labor

Synthesis $\dfrac{GDP_1 + GDP_2}{C_1 + V_1i + C_2 + V_2i}$ —general effectiveness

Scheme № 7

Dialectical Scheme of the Criteria of the Aggregate Effective Utilisation of Direct Labor in the Mass Media Sphere as a Whole (Formed on the Basis of Category «Net Domestic Product»)

Thesis $\dfrac{NDP_1 + NDP_2}{C_1 + C_2}$ —capital return

Antithesis $\dfrac{NDP_1 + NDP_2}{V_1i + V_2i}$ —productivity of a direct labor

Synthesis $\dfrac{NDP_1 + NDP_2}{C_1 + V_1i + C_2 + V_2i}$ —general effectiveness

Dialectical Scheme of the Criteria of the Aggregate Effective Utilisation of Direct Labor in the Mass Media Sphere as a Whole (Formed on the Basis of Category «Net Income»)

Thesis $\qquad \dfrac{m_1j + A^{MM}_{STP}k + m_2j}{C_1 + C_2}$ —capital return

Antithesis $\qquad \dfrac{m_1j + A^{MM}_{STP}k + m_2j}{V_1i + V_2i}$ —productivity of a direct labor

Synthesis $\qquad \dfrac{m_1j + A^{MM}_{STP}k + m_2j}{C_1 + V_1i + C_2 + V_2i}$ —general effectiveness

Dialectical Scheme of the Criteria of the Aggregate Effective Utilisation of Direct Labor in the Mass Media Sphere as Whole «Assimilated Resource Stp»)

Thesis $\qquad \dfrac{A^{MM}_{STP}k}{C_1 + C_2}$ —capital return

Antithesis $\qquad \dfrac{A^{MM}_{STP}k}{V_1i + V_2i}$ —productivity of a direct labor

Synthesis $\qquad \dfrac{A^{MM}_{STP}k}{C_1 + V_1i + C_2 + V_2i}$ —general effectiveness

In this chapter we consider the peculiarities of the investment indicators in the mass media sphere.

1) **_System of indicators of the «long-term effectiveness»_** of resource utilization in the mass media sphere formed on the basis of **_«Increment (Δ) of Gross Domestic Product» (GDP-MM)_** indicator:

$$\textbf{1. «Thesis» indicator} = \frac{\text{Increment } (\Delta)\ \text{GDP-MM}}{\text{Additional } (\Delta C)\ \text{past labor expenses}}$$

2. «Antithesis» indicator = $\dfrac{\text{Increment } (\Delta) \text{ GDP-MM}}{\text{Additional } (\Delta V) \text{ direct labor expenses}}$

3. «Synthesis» indicator = $\dfrac{\text{Increment } (\Delta) \text{ GDP-MM}}{\text{Additional aggregate labor expenses } (\Delta C + \Delta V)}$

2) ***System of indicators of the «long-term effectiveness»*** of resource utilization in the mass media sphere formed on the basis of ***«Increment (D) of Net Domestic Product» (NDP-MM)*** indicator:

1. «Thesis» indicator = $\dfrac{\text{Increment } (\Delta) \text{ NDP-MM}}{\text{Additional } (\Delta C) \text{ past labor expenses}}$

2. «Antithesis» indicator = $\dfrac{\text{Increment } (\Delta) \text{ NDP-MM}}{\text{Additional } (\Delta V) \text{ direct labor expenses}}$

3. «Synthesis» indicator = $\dfrac{\text{Increment } (\Delta) \text{ NDP-MM}}{\text{Additional aggregate labor expenses } (\Delta C + \Delta V)}$

3) ***System of indicators a of the «long-term effectiveness»*** of resource utilization in the mass media sphere formed on the basis of ***«Increment (D) of Net Income» (NI-MM)*** indicator:

1. «Thesis» indicator = $\dfrac{\text{Increment } (\Delta) \text{ NI-MM}}{\text{Additional } (\Delta C) \text{ past labor expenses}}$

2. «Antithesis» indicator = $\dfrac{\text{Increment } (\Delta) \text{ NI-MM}}{\text{Additional } (\Delta V) \text{ direct labor expenses}}$

3. «Synthesis» indicator = $\dfrac{\text{Increment } (\Delta) \text{ NI-MM}}{\text{Additional aggregate labor expenses } (\Delta C + \Delta V)}$

4) ***System of indicators of the «long-term effectiveness»*** of resource utilization in the mass media sphere formed on the basis of ***«Increment (D) of assimilated resource STP» (AR-STR)*** indicator:

1. «Thesis» indicator $= \dfrac{\text{Increment } (\Delta) \text{ AR-STR}}{\text{Additional } (\Delta C) \text{ past labor expenses}}$

2. «Antithesis» indicator $= \dfrac{\text{Increment } (\Delta) \text{ AR-STR}}{\text{Additional } (\Delta V) \text{ direct labor expenses}}$

3. «Synthesis» indicator $= \dfrac{\text{Increment } (\Delta) \text{ AR-STR}}{\text{Additional aggregate labor expenses } (\Delta C + \Delta V)}$

Now we would consider some of the peculiarities of the above given criteria of the «long-term effectiveness».

<u>***Scheme № 10***</u>

Aggregate Logical Scheme of the Indicator of the «Long-Term Effective Utilisation of Past Labour » in the Mass Media Sphere as a Whole (Formed on the Basis of Category «An Increment (Δ) of Gross Domestic Product»)

A) **Logical Scheme of the Indicator of the «Long-Term Effective Utilisation of Past Labour» in Division I**

Thesis	Increment (Δ) of the GDP-MM Division I $(\Delta C_1 + \Delta m_1 i + \Delta V_1 j)$
Antithesis	Additional (Δ) past labor expenses in Division I (ΔC_1)
Synthesis	$\dfrac{\Delta C_1 + \Delta m_1 i + \Delta V_1 j}{\Delta C_1}$

B) **Logical Scheme of the Indicator of the «Long-Term Effective Utilisation of Past Labour» in Division II**

Thesis	Increment (Δ) of the GDP-MM Division II $(\Delta C_2 + \Delta V_2 i + \Delta A^{MM}_{STP} k + \Delta m_2 j)$
Antithesis	Additional (Δ) past labor expenses in Division II (ΔC_2)
Synthesis	$\dfrac{\Delta C_2 + \Delta V_2 i + \Delta A^{MM}_{STP} k + \Delta m_2 j}{\Delta C_2}$

C) Logical Scheme of the Indicator of the «Long-Term Effective Utilisation of Past Labour» in Divisions I & II

Thesis

Increment (Δ) of the GDP-ED-SP Divisions I & II
$$\Delta C_1 + \Delta V_1 i + \Delta m_1 j + \Delta C_2 + \Delta V_2 i + \Delta m_2 j + \Delta A^{MM}_{STP} k$$

Antithesis

Additional (Δ) past labor expenses in Divisions I & II
$$(\Delta C_1 + \Delta C_2)$$

Synthesis

$$\frac{\Delta C_1 + \Delta V_1 i + \Delta m_1 j + \Delta C_2 + \Delta V_2 i + \Delta m_2 j + \Delta A^{MM}_{STP} k}{\Delta C_1 + \Delta C_2}$$

The Macroeconomy of the Internet Sphere

In the economy of the Internet sphere there is quite number of problems that need to be solved. Judge for yourselves:

- until recently, the Internet sphere has never been examined as an economic system;
- peculiarities of the Internet components haven't been worked out;
- peculiarities of the economic relations in the Internet sphere haven't been defined;
- essence of the categories—Internet value, Internet services, complex Internet product—hasn't been established;
- economic estimations of the Internet values are defined separately from the economic estimations of the Internet services;
- «On Line Time» (OLT) is not considered as an economic resource;
- the OLT resource is not included in the cost of the Internet services;
- specific features of the economic estimations connected with the movement of the Internet values and Internet services.

The economic criteria of the effectiveness of the use of resources in the framework of production, distribution, exchange and consumption have not been explained.

The outlines of these problems become clearer and significantly better understood if Internet values, Internet services and the OLT are examined in a three-dimensional space.

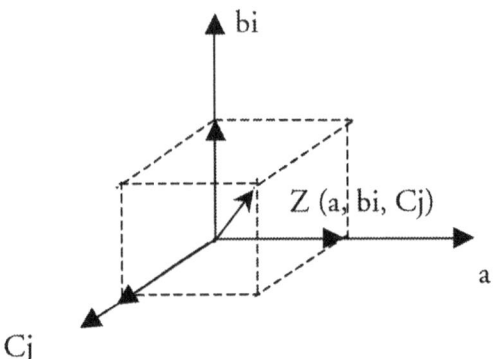

where

    (a) is the cost estimation of Internet values (computers, programmes etc.)

    (bi) represents the expenses connected with the creation of Internet services (OLT not included)

    (Cj) is the cost estimation of the assimilated OLT resource.

The total vector z is formulated as follows: $Z = a + bi + Cj$

The z vector assumes different values depending on the three components a, b and c.

If the particular OLT resource is not taken into account, the Z vector is being examined in two-dimensional space, without the Cj component.

If we look at the reproduction of the Internet sphere from this position, i.e. without the «On Line Time» (OLT) resource, it will mean that one of the basic Internet incoming resources is excluded. As a result, the economic estimations are decreased by the amount of not included OLT resource.

In the diagrams of the reproduction of the Internet sphere the following takes place:

    -   equalities between separate parts of the Internet values and Internet services (in the multibillion calculation) without taking into account the OLT resource become inequalities.

    -   inequalities, compiled without taking into account the OLT resource, become equalities for the same reason.

How is it possible to examine the process of the exchange of Internet values and Internet services on a macroeconomic level without taking into account the

OLT resource, when the annual multibillion volume of the Internet values and Internet services is exchanged with another multibillion volume of values and services?

The exchange process may be explained only with real economic estimations, which include the OLT resource. Then you can see relationship existing between the internal parts of the Internet products in the annual reproduction process.

Some Internet researchers propose to examine the function of «demand and supply». This approach is taken from the theory of material production.

The deficiency of this approach is that it examines two types of relations: «production» and «consumption». In other words, in theory, a specific «surgical operation» is performed to remove two economic relationships: «distribution» and «exchange» in the Internet sphere.

In the square outlined by dashes I have shown the part of the relationship that is cut out.

Production	Distribution	Exchange	Consumption
A. «Production» process of Internet values →	«Distribution» process of Internet values →	«Exchange» process of Internet values →	«Consumption» process of Internet values
↓	↓	↓	↓
B. «Production» process of Internet services →	«Distribution» process of Internet services →	«Exchange» process of Internet services →	«Consumption» process of Internet services
↓	↓	↓	↓
C. «Production» process of complex Internet product →	«Distribution» process of complex Internet product →	«Exchange» process of complex Internet product →	«Consumption» process of complex Internet product

After the above «surgical operation» only two types of relationships will remain:

Production		Consumption
A.	«Production» process of Internet values	→	«Consumption» process of Internet values
	↓		↓
B.	«Production» process of Internet services	→	«Consumption» process of Internet services
	↓		↓
C.	«Production» process of complex Internet product	→	«Consumption» process of complex Internet product

Can we understand the economic issues of the Internet sphere if we only examine the production and consumption of Internet values and Internet services?

If we examine the economic relationships of the Internet in its curtailed form then the following processes will remain unconsidered:

Distribution		Exchange
A.	«Distribution» process of Internet values	→	«Exchange» process of Internet values
	↓		↓
B.	«Distribution» process of Internet services	→	«Exchange» process of Internet services
	↓		↓
C.	«Distribution» process of complex Internet product	→	«Exchange» process of complex Internet product

Without taking into consideration the relationship of «distribution» and «exchange» it is impossible to understand the whole process of movement of Internet values and Internet services.

Definitely, research cannot be confined to the framework of the two relationships. This is not sufficient for the understanding of the economic processes that take place on the Internet sphere. This is a gross logical mistake.

The economic relationships of the Internet are interconnected. Each one of the economic relationships forms part of the common reproduction process and has its own specific characteristics:

- characteristics of the production of Internet values and Internet services;
- characteristics of the distribution of Internet values and Internet services;
- characteristics of the exchange of Internet values and Internet services;
- characteristics of the consumption of Internet values and Internet services.

When studying economic relationships we must:

- reject the old, petty dogmas of theory, which prevent us from moving forward;
- choose logical methods, which will be used in Internet theory;
- select numbers are going to use when calculating the expenditures and results of the Internet sphere;
- we should not compile a theory of the Internet sphere, by using only one or two economic relationships.

Complex Approach to Research of Economic Processes

1. **Logic Approach to Research of Social Production**
2. **«Number» as Instrument of Research for Economic Processes**
3. **Definition of the Complex Number**
4. **Operations on Complex Numbers in Algebraic Form**

Complex Approach to Research of Economic Processes

If to assume that economic processes and economic relations are complex; economic interests are complex; social relations are complex then in the research of complex economic and social processes it is necessary to use a complex approach, together with complex knowledge, complex instruments and complex numbers. This is proven.[29]

In this logical sequence everything corresponds with each other. There are no defects. Everything is the way it should be.

We should not try to attempt avoiding the complex line. We should follow it everywhere. If we do not do it, the approach will be different from the complex one; it will not be complex.

The essence of the complex approach, from my point of view, is in application of the following:

1. Logic—dialectical method with categories: thesis, antithesis, synthesis;
   - inductive method;
   - deductive method etc.
2. Logical operations—operative system of formal logic;
3. Numbers—as an instrument of representing economic (social) processes;
4. Operations with numbers (technology of using numbers).

Depending on the kind of numbers used in economic processes, a complex approach can be modified in several different ways.

---

[29]   The economic processes (social process) represent:

Thesis   Positive tendency in the process

Antithesis Negative tendency in the process

Synthesis   Process in its entity (interactive process of positive and negative tendencies)

Peculiarities of Complex Approach to Research of Economic Processes (With the Use of Natural Numbers)

1. Logic—dialectical method with categories: thesis, antithesis, synthesis;
   - inductive method;
   - deductive method etc.
2. Logical operations—operative system of formal logic;
3. Natural numbers—as an instrument, (mirror) representing economic processes
4. Operations with natural numbers (technology № 1).

Peculiarities of Complex Approach to Research of Economic Processes (With the Use of Real Numbers)

1. Logic—dialectical method with categories: thesis, antithesis, synthesis;
   - inductive method;
   - deductive method etc.
2. Logical operations—operative system of formal logic;
3. Real numbers—as an instrument, (mirror) reflecting economic processes
4. Operations using real numbers (technology № 2).

Peculiarities of Complex Approach to Research of Economic Processes (With the Use of Irrational Numbers)

1. Logic—dialectical method with categories: thesis, antithesis, synthesis;
   - inductive method;
   - deductive method etc.
2. Logical operations—operative system of formal logic;
3. Irrational numbers—as an instrument (mirror) reflecting economic processes
4. Operations with irrational numbers (technology № 3).

Peculiarities of Complex Approach to
Research of Economic Processes
(With the Use of Complex Numbers)

1. Logic—dialectical method with categories: thesis, antithesis, synthesis;

    -   inductive method;

    -   deductive method etc.

2. Logical operations—operative system of formal logic;

3. Complex numbers—as an instrument (mirror) reflecting economic processes

4. Operations with complex numbers (technology № 4).

Research of economic processes, which take place in the Internet sphere, requires not only knowledge but also an ability to use a certain «surgical instrument» in the capacity of which numbers are represented. Mathematical calculations occur in the quality of technology related to the usage of the numbers.

Doing my research of the Internet economic processes, I concentrated on three variants:

Variant I

-   dialectic method

-   logical operations

-   real numbers

-   mathematical operations using real numbers[30]

Variant II

-   dialectic method

-   logical operations

-   complex numbers

-   mathematical operations with complex numbers

Variant III

-   dialectic method

-   logical operations

---

[30]   This variant has been analysed in the book «Internet Sphere Economy»

- quaternions
- mathematical operations with numbers—quaternions

In the first variant simple mathematical operations are used. In the second variant the operations are a bit more complex. In the third variant the operations are very complex.

The results achieved using these three variants differ one from the other.

Every system of calculation has its virtues and vices.

2. «Number» as Instrument of Research of Economic Processes

In the hall of mirrors which we all visited one time or the other in our childhood, the mirrors' surfaces were distorted: some of them were convex, others concave. That affected our reflection in the mirror. These various transformations entertained us. Of course, it was funny.

I have mentioned the hall of mirrors in connection with different numbers the fact that a researcher of the economic processes who uses in his research—natural, irrational, real, imaginary, compound and super-compound (quaternions)—finds himself in an analogous situation. The numbers can be treated as a specific mirror that reflects economic processes.

Numbers, numbers, numbers—they are present everywhere, both in traditional and untraditional economy.

We don't ponder on the kind of numbers we use in economic calculations, although a lot depends on them. Real numbers reflect one depth of the economic processes; imaginary numbers show the other.

We should not be afraid of using untraditional numbers. If we look realistically, we can see that social sciences meet with exact sciences and they «go together»—next to real numbers, imaginary numbers and complex numbers quaternions.

Researching economic processes, we should not be afraid of fresh ideas and new horizons. Both in the area of the traditional and—even more importantly—untraditional economy, we should not find ourselves in the zone of old approaches, old opinions, thoughts and definitions.

It has taken thousands of years to define numbers. The numbers' theory has been widening and developing. For example, the ancient Greek mathematicians thought that only natural numbers were real.

In the times of Pythagoras a discovery was made in the area of numbers. Its essence consisted in the fact that there were not enough natural numbers, if one tried to put into practice the arithmetic calculations connected with the diagonal of a square (see Pythagorean Theory). There, the necessity of using real numbers came up.

I am not going to go deeper into the theory of the development of numbers' definition. It is enough if I say that <u>in our daily life we use real numbers and basic arithmetic calculations such as addition, subtraction, multiplication and division</u>. Only in some exceptional situation, do we raise a number to the nth power or extract the square root. In other words, <u>we use one type of numbers (real) and primitive mathematical apparatus (in our daily life)</u>.

If we raise (A + B) to the third, fourth power, some very complex problems arise. Their essence consists in the fact that there are not enough real numbers (the ones that we use in our daily life) to solve the equations. Part of the equations can be solved only with the utilisation of <u>complex numbers</u>.

This situation partly explains the necessity of using new numbers and new methods of technology in calculations. There, everything looks the same as in daily life: some things can be measured by a simple ruler, some only using a logarithmic ruler. This is clear for everybody.

Because of this, mathematicians give the following example. <u>The system of the simple equations does not have a solution in the framework of real numbers,</u>

$$\begin{cases} X + Y = 10 \\ X \cdot Y = 40 \end{cases}$$

This system of equations looks simple. But the solutions for these equations lie beyond the borders of real numbers. Beyond the border of existing, traditional definitions, opinions and axioms. If we cross the line of «impossibility» imposed on us by real numbers, we will find solutions, but the journey towards these solutions leads through an arithmetically impossible operation—extracting the square root of negative number. The solution of the equation is as follows:

$$X = 5 \pm\sqrt{-15}; Y = 5 \pm\sqrt{-15}$$

3. Definition of the Complex Numbers

In 1545 Italian mathematician G. Cardano made the first steps towards development of a theory of complex numbers.

1n 1572 R. Bombelli established rules of an arithmetic operation on numbers.

In 1637 R. Decart offered a name for new numbers—«imaginary numbers».

In 1831 K.Gauss introduced a concept of an imaginary unity.

In the list of those who worked out complex numbers there are many well-known names—G. LaGrange, P.Laplas, Y.Bernulli, K.Vessel, G.Argan, and W.Hamilton.

The scope of usage of complex numbers is expanding with every passing year.

Complex numbers have incorporated the logic of the dialectical method.

Dialectic logic of construction of complex numbers.

Thesis	Real numbers—«a»
Antithesis	Imaginary number—«bi»
Synthesis	Complex number—Z = «a + bi»

The principal feature, being at the same time its advantage, of the «complex number» (complexus) is that with the help of complex numbers it is possible to reveal combination of several concepts, phenomena and processes as a whole. That is, the complex number reveals the idea of compositions of concepts, compositions of processes and compositions of phenomena.

Definition 1. Numbers—$a + bi$, where a and b—are real numbers, i—an imaginary unit—we will call them complex numbers.

Number a we will call a real part of a complex number, bi—an imaginary part of a complex number, b—a factor at an imaginary part. There are cases when it is possible that real numbers are equal to zero. If $a = 0$, a complex number bi refers to only imaginary. If $b = 0$, a complex number a + bi is equal to a and refers to only real. If $a = 0$ and $b = 0$ simultaneously, a complex number $a + bi$ is equal to zero. So, we have got that real numbers and only imaginary numbers are special cases of a complex number.

Record of a complex number as $a + bi$ is called an algebraic form of a complex number.

A complex number is represented either as a point with coordinates (a, b) or as a vector beginning in the center of coordinates (0,0) and ending in the point with coordinates (a, b) (see fig. 1).

Axis X is called a real axis, axis Y—an imaginary axis and a plane Z itself—a plane of complex numbers or Z-plane. Real numbers can be represented by points of a direct line as it is shown in figure 1.

Segments OA OB, can also represent these numbers, taking into account not only their length but the direction as well.

Imaginary axis

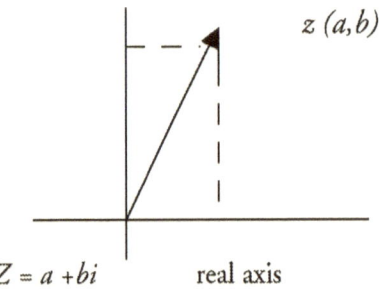

z (a,b)

$Z = a + bi$ real axis

Two complex numbers $a + bi$ and $c + di$ are considered equal in only case when separately their real parts and factors at imaginary unit one are equal, that is $a + bi = c + di$, if $a = c$ and $b = d$.

4. Operations on Complex Numbers in Algebraic Form

Addition, subtraction, multiplication of complex numbers in algebraic form are carried out according to the rules of corresponding operations on multinomial.

a) $z_1 + z_2 = (a_1 + b_1 i) + (a_2 + b_2 i) = (a_1 + a_2) + (b_1 i + b_2 i)$

b) $z_1 - z_2 = (a_1 + b_1 i) - (a_2 + b_2 i) = (a_1 - a_2) + (b_1 i - b_2 i)$

c) $z_1 z_2 = (a_1 + b_1 i) \times (a_2 + b_2 i) = a_1 a_2 + a_1 b_2 i + a_2 b_1 i + b_1 b_2 i^2 = a_1 a_2 + a_1 b_2 i + a_2 b_1 i - b_1 b_2 = (a_1 a_2 - b_1 b_2) + (a_1 b_2 + a_2 b_1)i$

d)

$$\frac{z_1}{z_2} = \frac{a_1a_2 + b_1b_2}{a_2^2 + b_2^2} + \frac{a_2b_1 - a_1b_2}{a_2^2 + b_2^2}$$

P.S.

Many countries have just begun the path towards democratic reorganizations.

In a vast number of countries clan relations predominate. Somewhere elders still exist, as they did 300-400 years ago.

«Democracy» is a difficult category which should be considered from the logic side, philosophic side and economic side.

ATTACHMENT 2

Operations with Complex Numbers in Algebraic Form

1) Geometric Interpretation of a Complex Number

A complex number $Z = a + bi$ can be shown by point Z of the plane with coordinates (a; b) (pic. 1). For this purpose let's choose on the plane Decart's rectangular system of coordinates. Real numbers are shown by points of abscissa axis, which is called a real (or material) axis; purely imaginary numbers—by points of ordinate axis, which we will call an imaginary axis. To each point of plane with coordinates (a; b) corresponds one and only one vector starting at 0 (0; 0) and ending in Z (a; b). So a complex number $Z = a + bi$ can be represented as a vector c starting at point 0 (0; 0) and ending at point Z (a; b).

Example 8. Represent on a plane numbers $z = 5$; $z = 3i$; $z = 3 + 2i$; $z = 5 - 2i$; $z = -3 + 2i$; $z = -1 - 5i$.

Solution. Given numbers are shown in figure 2.

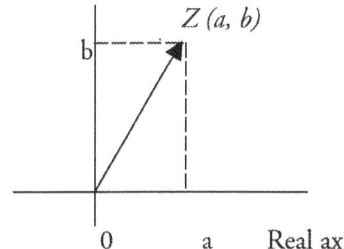

Fig. 1

2) Concept of an Imaginary Unity

Let us assume that there is such a number, which square is equal to - *1*. We designate this number by letter i; then we can record: $i^2 = - 1$.

Number *i* we will call an imaginary number (*i*—an initial letter of the French word—imaginaire—«imaginary»), and the previous equation we will consider a definition of an imaginary unit.

From this equation we find i = $\sqrt{-1}$

Introduction of an imaginary unit allows us now to extract square roots from negative numbers.

For example

$$\sqrt{-36} = \sqrt{36 \bullet (-1)} = \sqrt{36} \bullet \sqrt{-1} = 6i$$

$$\sqrt{-\frac{1}{4}} = \sqrt{\frac{1}{4} \bullet (-1)} = \sqrt{\frac{1}{4}} \bullet \sqrt{-1} = \frac{1}{2}i$$

3) Power of Imaginary Unit

Let us examine the powers of imaginary unit:

i;

$i^2 = - 1$;

$i^3 = i^2 \cdot i = (- 1)i = - i$;

$i^4 = i^3 \cdot i = - i \cdot i = - i^2 = - (- 1) = 1$;

$i^5 = i^4 \cdot i = 1 \cdot i = i$;

$i^6 = i^5 \cdot i = i \cdot i = i^2 = - 1$;

$i^7 = i^6 \cdot i = (- 1) \cdot i = - i$;

$i^8 = i^7 \cdot i = - i \cdot i = 1$;

If we write out all values of the number *i* power we shall receive the following sequence: *i, -1, -i, 1, i, -1, -i, i* etc. It is easy to notice that the values of the number i power reoccur at a period equal to 4.

Thus $i = i$, $i^2 = -1$, $i^3 = -i$, $i^4 = 1$, $i^5 = i$, $i^6 = -1$, $i^7 = -i$, $i^8 = 1$, $i^9 = i$, $i^{10} = -1$, i^{11} $= -i$, $i^{12} = i$.

Thus, if the index of power of number i is divided into 4, the value of the power equals 1, if at the division of power index into 4 the remainder comes to 1, the index of value makes i; if at the division of power value into 4 the remainder comes to 2, the value of power equals 1; and lastly if at the division into 4 the remainder is 3, the value of power is equal i. Using this we can calculate any power of the number i. Example. Find i^{28}; i^{33}; $i^{135} = -i$.

4. Operations on Complex Numbers in Algebraic Form

Addition, subtraction, multiplication of complex numbers in algebraic form are carried out according to the rules of corresponding operations on multinomial.

Example 1. Complex numbers are given $z_1 = 2 + 3i$, $z_2 = 5 - 7i$. Find:

a) $z_1 + z_2$

$z_1 + z_2 = (2 + 3i) + (5 - 7i) = 2 + 3i + 5 - 7i = (2 + 5) + (3i - 7i) = 7 - 4i$;

b) $z_1 - z_2$

$z_1 - z_2 = (2 + 3i) - (5 - 7i) = 2 + 3i - 5 + 7i = (2 - 5) + (3i + 7i) = -3 + 10$;

c) $z_1 z_2$

$z_1 z_2 = (2 + 3i)(5 - 7i) = 10 - 14i + 15i - 21i^2 = 10 - 14i + 15i + 21 = (10 + 21) + (-14i + 15i) = 31 + i$

(with $i^2 = -1$ taken into account here).

Solution.

Note. At carrying out multiplication the following formulas can be used:

$(a \pm b)^2 = a^2 \pm 2ab + b^2$,

$(a \pm b)^3 = a^3 \pm 3a^2b + 3ab \pm b^3$.

Example 2. Perform operations:

a) $(2 + 3i)^2$;   б) $(3 - 5i)^2$;   в) $(5 + 3i)^3$.

Solution.

a) $(2 + 3i)^2 = 4 + 2 \times 2 \times 3i + 9i^2 = 4 + 12i - 9 = -5 + 12i$;

б) $(3 - 5i)^2 = 9 - 2 \times 3 \times 5i + 25i^2 = 9 - 30i - 25 = -16 - 30i;$

в) $(5 + 3i)^3 = 125 + 3 \times 25 \times 3i + 3 \times 5 \times 9i^2 + 27i^3;$
    since $i^2 = -1$, and $i^3 = -i$, we have $(5 + 3i)^3 = 125 + 225i - 135 - 27i = -10 + 198i.$

We shall consider the usage of formula now.

$(a + b)(a - b) = a^2 - b^2.$

Example 3. Perform operations:

a) $(5 + 3i)(5 - 3i);$

б) $(2 + 5i)(2 - 5i);$

в) $(1 + i)(1 - i).$

Solution

a) $(5 + 3i)(5 - 3i) = 5^2 - (3i)^2 = 25 - 9i^2 = 25 + 9 = 34;$

б) $(2 + 5i)(2 - 5i) = 2^2 - (5i)^2 = 4 + 25 = 29;$

в) $(1 + i)(1 - i) = 1^2 - i^2 = 1 + 1 = 2.$

Note that while using Formula (*) we always receive a particular case of the complex number—real number, and complex number that we multiply are conjugated.

Definition 2. Two complex numbers are considered to be conjugated if they are distinguished only by values placed before the imaginary part.

We see that the product of two conjugated numbers is always equal to real number. We can use this quality to perform the division of two complex numbers. To carry out division we perform an additional operation: multiply dividend and factor by complex number conjugated with factor.

Example 4. Perform the division:

a) $\dfrac{2 + 3i}{5 - 7i}$ b) $\dfrac{3 + 5i}{2 + 6i}$

Solution.

a) We have

$$\frac{2+3i}{5-7i} = \frac{(2+3i)(5+7i)}{(5-7i)(5+7i)}$$

Perform multiplications for the dividend and the factor separately:

$(2 + 3i)(5 + 7i) = 10 + 14i + 15i + 21i^2 = - 11 + 29i;$
$(5 - 7i)(5 + 7i) = 25 - 49i^2 = 25 + 49 = 74.$

Thus,

a) $\dfrac{2+3i}{5-7i} = \dfrac{(2+3i)(5+7i)}{(5-7i)(5+7i)} = \dfrac{-11+29i}{74} = -\dfrac{11}{74} + \dfrac{29}{74}i;$

b) $\dfrac{3+5i}{2+6i} = \dfrac{(3+5i)(2-6i)}{(2+6i)(2-6i)} = \dfrac{6-18i+10i-30i^2}{4-36i^2}$
$= \dfrac{36-8i}{40} = \dfrac{9}{10} - \dfrac{1}{5}i$

Now we shall consider the solution of square equations with negative discriminant:

Example 5. Find the discriminant according to the formula: $D = b^2 - 4ac.$
a) $x^2 - 6x + 13 = 0;$ б) $9x^2 + 12x + 29 = 0.$

Since $a = 1, b = - 6, c = 13,$
$D = (- 6)^2 - 4 \cdot 1 \cdot 13 = 36 - 52 = - 16;$
$\sqrt{D} = \sqrt{-16} = \sqrt{16 \bullet (-1)} = 4i$

We find the roots of the equations according to formulas

$$x_1 = \frac{-b-\sqrt{D}}{2a}; \quad x_2 = \frac{-b-\sqrt{D}}{2a}$$

$$x_1 = \frac{6 - 4i}{2} = \frac{2(3 + 2i)}{2} = 3 - 2i$$

$$x_2 = \frac{6 + 4i}{2} = \frac{2(3 + 2i)}{2} = 3 + 2i$$

b)   Here $a = 9$, $b = 12$, $c = 29$. Thus,

$$D = b^2 - 4ac = 12^2 - 4 \cdot 9 \cdot 29 = 144 - 1044 = -900,$$

$$\sqrt{D} = \sqrt{-900} = \sqrt{900 \cdot (-1)} = 30i$$

We find the roots of the equation:

$$x_1 = \frac{-12 - 30i}{18} = \frac{6(-2 - 5i)}{18} = \frac{-2 - 5i}{3} = -\frac{2}{3} - \frac{5}{3}i$$

$$x_1 = \frac{-12 + 30i}{18} = \frac{6(-2 + 5i)}{18} = \frac{-2 + 5i}{3} = -\frac{2}{3} + \frac{5}{3}i$$

We can see that if the descriminant of the square equation is negative, then the square equation has two conjugated roots.

978-0-595-44128-0
0-595-44128-9

www.ingramcontent.com/pod-product-compliance
Lightning Source LLC
Chambersburg PA
CBHW022253290526
45785CB00015B/750